HORSE SENSE

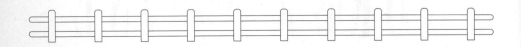

Jockey Victor Espinoza and War Emblem conclude "the most famous two minutes in racing," the 2002 Kentucky Derby *(Getty Images, Getty Images North America).*

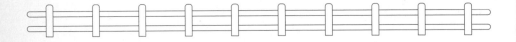

HORSE SENSE

An Inside Look at the Sport of Kings

Bert Sugar

with

Cornell Richardson

WILEY

JOHN WILEY & SONS, INC.

This book is dedicated to the millions—owners,
trainers, jockeys, and "improvers of the breed,"
also known as bettors—who have remade
"The Sport of Kings"
into
"The King of Sports."

CONTENTS

FOREWORD

Behind Bert Sugar's trademark fedora that looks like a throwback to the Ben Hechtian "Front Page" days of the '30s and '40s, and that omnipresent Groucho Marx (or is it Churchill's?) cigar, behind the chain-joking television personality that seems to be laughing and highballing through life is the serious sports historian who now adds *Horse Sense* to his five-foot shelf of sporting life literature.

If horse racing is the Sport of Kings, with racing stables the playthings of the very rich, the Belmonts, Whitneys, and Vanderbilts, the Kentucky aristocracy and the sultans and Ahmeds-come-lately, Mr. Sugar informs us—with colorful examples—that it's also the province of the bargain hunter who buys the legendary Man o' War for $5,000, or the great Seattle Slew for $17,500, while, year after year, million-dollar yearlings never make it to a stakes race. Buying these baby racehorses, no matter how royal their bloodlines, is still, we learn, a case of "Hey, ya never know!"

The Sport of Kings, Bert Sugar reminds us in his appropriately racy prose, is also the sport of the two-dollar bettor. You don't have to be sitting up there on Churchill Downs's "Millionaires'

Row" to feel a glowing proprietorship in a winning horse. A humble mutuel ticket at the window puts you at that table as you cheer your four-legged hunch to his win by a nostril at the wire, or tear up your ticket in momentary despair.

How that horse is bred, how he (or she) has been trained, how ridden, how syndicated (for more money than ever earned at the track), why some great horses sire other great horses while other champions strike out as studs, the roll-call of unforgettable characters from owners to trainers to jockeys to the horses themselves— the whole mystique of this addictive sport is spelled out for you in a book that lives up to its subtitle, *"An Inside Look . . . ."*

Before you hurry off to Belmont, Hialeah, or Hollywood Park, or to your nearest OTB parlor, you've got a winner with your ticket to *Horse Sense.*

BUD SCHULBERG
Author, Academy Award
Winner, *On the Waterfront*

ACKNOWLEDGMENTS

Like Dimitri Tiomkin, who, in accepting the Oscar for best musical score in 1952 for *High Noon*, thanked "Shostakovich, Tchaikovsky, Rimsky-Korsakov, and Prokofiev," we, too, would like to thank those whose shoulders we stood upon in writing *Horse Sense*. They include, in no particular order: Walter Haight, Red Smith, and Jim Murray, all giants in the world of writing, who shared their knowledge and stories with us in a previous movie; another giant, Jimmy Breslin, who took the time to fill in some holes that would have gone a-begging without his help; owner Giles Brophy, who took us, step-by-step, through the convoluted world of auctions; Dave "Down the Stretch They Come" Johnson, whose knowledge of racing is exceeded only by his live race calls; Tim Smith and Eric Wing of the National Thoroughbred Racing Association, and Melinda Markey Van Dyke and Alec Mackenzie, all of whom encouraged us in this work; Warren "The Silver Fox" Fisher, who has covered every racetrack from Worcester, Massachusetts, to El Comandante in San Juan, and who was extremely helpful in the completion of this book; the Keeneland Library and its two librarians, Phyllis Rogers and Cathy Schenck, both of whom helped point fuzzy brains in the right direction; the *Daily Racing Form* and *Thoroughbred Times* Internet Archives; Fran Buonarota, Suzy Sugar, and Brian Ash, who convinced us that dangling participles never raced in the fifth at Santa Anita and earned medals, with oak leaf clusters, for having the patience to put up with us; Matt Holt, senior editor, and Maureen Drexel, production manager, over at John Wiley & Sons, Inc., who carried us longer than our mothers; and especially Budd Schulberg, who graciously and gracefully wrote the foreword, and the great sports artist LeRoy Neiman, who provided the exceptional artwork. We thank them all, for without them there would have been no book.

PUBLISHER'S ACKNOWLEDGMENTS

We extend thanks to the following persons for their assistance in the editing and production of this title: Linda Witzling, senior production manager and Tamara Hummel, editorial assistant, at John Wiley & Sons, Inc., for production guidance and research contributions, respectively. We are grateful to Nancy Marcus Land and Pam Blackmon, our production team at Publications Development Company of Texas, for composition and design contributions throughout the project. We also thank Barbara Hanson and John Drexel for their copyediting and research expertise. Finally, we express our appreciation to Anthony Sullivan and Eric Smalkin of Getty Images for their assistance in obtaining the photographs for *Horse Sense*.

HORSE SENSE

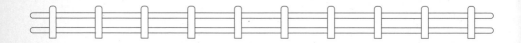

Derby at Epsom *(Copyright © Hulton Archive).*

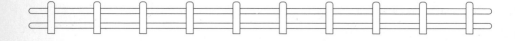

INTRODUCTION

When songwriters pose the musical question, "What is this thing called love?" some in the audience will answer it's the "thing" you find in potboilers where boy meets girl, boy loses girl, boy finally gets girl. Others, a mutual admiration society consisting of two members, which makes the world go round, usually when it should be asleep. And, the more cynical, the tenth word in a telegram.

For hundreds of thousands of others "that thing called love" is the love affair that we have with horses, one which goes back almost to the time Father Adam first heard the stampede of the apple peddlers. Not merely the kind of love you find at the windows where affection flows at $2 a heartbeat—minus, as Red Smith said, taxes, take, and breakage—but one experienced by many who wouldn't know a finish line from a furlong.

The effect horses have on those who fall in love with them can be attributed to many things, almost in a let-us-count-the-ways list: their noble and majestic bearing; their elegance and eloquence in movement; their grace, speed, and beauty; their personality; or their mere size. Whatever the reason, it falls some-where in the line alternately attributed to Sir Winston Churchill, Oscar Wilde, or George Bernard Shaw (and probably, by modern members of the Bartlett Society, to Yogi Berra) which goes: "There is something about the outside of a horse that is good for the inside of man."

Once upon a time, the horse was a beast of draft, not burden, moving man's articles of commerce from one place to an-other, their ponylike size too small to support a man. As horses evolved in size, they were employed to pull chariots, first in war-fare and then in Ben Hur-like competitions—chariot races were part of the first Olympiad in 776 B.C. It wasn't until two centuries later that horse-running races, with riders on horses' backs, be-came part of the Olympics.

"Horses soon dominated the mind of the early races, especially of the Mediterranean," wrote D(avid) H(erbert) Lawrence. "You were a lord if you had a horse," Lawrence went on, pointing out that King Suppiluliumas of Mitanni, a part of Mesopotamia, had royal trotters, which were the world's first documented racehorses.

The Arabs were the first to employ selective breeding to pro-duce better horses and, as early as the twelfth century, some of those horses began to turn up in England, as English knights re-turned from the Crusades with horses appropriated from Arab lands. Over the next 400 years, an increasing number of Arabian stallions were imported and bred to English mares, with the end product being a horse possessing both speed and endurance. Matching the fastest of those animals in two-horse races for private wagers became a popular diversion of nobility, with King Richard the Lion-Hearted credited with issuing the first victory purse.

Yellowing records found amongst the royal papers by eagle-eyed racing archeologists indicate that something approaching modern racing began somewhere during the reign of Henry VIII, probably as early as 1511. It gained recognition as a professional sport two centuries later during the reign of Queen Anne, when match racing gave way to racing involving several horses on which the so-called *fancy* of the time placed wagers. Records also disclose that in the early 1700s the Duke of Devonshire owned what most English horse fanciers call the greatest race horse that ever lived, The Flying Childers, who was unbeaten—even once carrying nine stone (126 pounds) and running three-and-a half miles in six minutes and forty seconds, a record never approached—and sired a total of 497 winners.

Soon race courses began to dot the English landscape and, with the proliferation of courses and the rapid expansion of the sport, came the need for a central governing authority. In 1750, England's elite met at Newmarket to form the Jockey Club, which wrote rules, sanctioned race courses, and established standards that exist today.

Meanwhile, on this side of the pond, thoroughbred racing was introduced to the Colonies by a few prominent settlers who brought their horses and their love of racing to the New World, laying out the first American track on Long Island as early as 1665. The English connection continued when some American horse fanciers bought the winner of the inaugural 1780 English

Derby, Diomed, so little thought of in England that, by the age of twenty-two, he was consigned to the task of pulling a wagon and was purchased for the slight sum of £50, or $250, and brought over to the States to stand at stud.

According to biographers, George Washington was a regular attendee at races held at Annapolis and at a small race meet conducted in the Virginia panhandle by his brother, Charles—for whom the city of Charles Town was named—Washington also served as steward.

Several events drew huge crowds before the Civil War, including a match race between Fashion and Boston in 1842 at the Union Race Course on Long Island, won by Fashion and attended by 70,000 spectators, including forty United States senators and congressmen. And, a dozen years later, President Millard Fillmore and over 20,000 others witnessed the great horse Lexington defeat the previously unbeaten Lecomte in a two-heat match race at a track in New Orleans.

Still, horse racing was considered a sport only for the upper classes until after the Civil War.

The geographic divide of the Civil War (or "War of Northern Incursion," depending upon which side of the War you lived on), once waged with guns, was now carried on with horses, each section investing their horses with regional pride. The North counted among its horses those "freed" by conquering troops from Southern plantations as "spoils of war" and sold at auction, as were those taken from a plantation near Donaldson, Louisiana, sold to a purchaser who took them North in the name of "improvement in the breed for the Turf, the saddle and for general purposes." The

South, on the other hand, in an effort to re-create their antebellum ways, built "gentleman tracks" and restocked their horse farms.

By the beginning of the decade after Appomattox, the two sides took their Blue-Gray battle to the track, with Harry Bassett meeting Longfellow at Long Branch, New Jersey, to settle, at least in the hearts and pocketbooks of their followers, the dispute. Both animals had been bred in Kentucky, but, while Longfellow had been trained in the Bluegrass Country, Harry Bassett had been trained in New Jersey and was considered by his fans to represent the North. By the day of the race, the followers of the two horses were as divided as they had been five years earlier, with hundreds upon hundreds wagering their bottom dollars on *their* horse—depending upon their side of the Mason-Dixon Line. Although Harry Bassett went off as the betting favorite, there being more Northern money available than Southern, Longfellow finished over 100 yards to the good in the two-and-a-half mile race, insuring that hundreds of racing fans would not have to walk home to Dixie.

The North-South track debate spawned others, with several variations on the theme. In 1876, the great mare Mollie McCarthy was sent all the way from Sacramento to Louisville to measure strides with the pride of Kentucky, Ten Broeck, in a four-mile match race. The Kentucky colt, withstanding the early speed of the California mare, came on and won as he pleased, prompting the Californians to venture that had but the race been a shorter one she would have won. The Kentucky fans of Ten Broeck responded: "It ain't speed that wins horse races, it's staying power and bottom that turns the trick."

At Monmouth Race Course in 1885, another great race was set up to settle sectional differences pitting Freeland, "The Grandest Hoss in the Land," owned by Ed Corrigan of Chicago, against Miss Woodford, known as "The Queen of the Turf," owned by the Dwyer Brothers of Brooklyn. The rivalry was such that the Dwyer Brothers, offering 5 to 4 on their mare, bet the western crowd to a standstill. With two of the greatest jockeys of the day, Jimmy McLaughlin and Isaac Murphy, aboard the two, the race was described by Dick Cary, better known as "Hyder Ali" to readers of his Sporting Ballads, in this breathless manner:

> You know the rest, as the books you have read
> How McLaughlin kept the brown mare ahead
> Till Freeland came with a sudden dart
> At the finish, and Isaac proved too smart
> For the Dwyers' jock; how at the last
> He nailed him just as the post was passed,
> Oh, I tell you it was a close-run race,
> And it gave to Murphy the pride of place.

Other great late-nineteenth-century sectional rivalries were played out on the track as well, with Yo Tambien from Chicago racing against Ray S., the horse of the Fleischmanns of Cincinnati, for Midwest supremacy; the western-owned Colonial Girl against the great eastern horse Hermis; and what was then called the great eastern *crack* Domino against the California-owned and bred Rey El Santa Anita in the American Derby.

While all these sectional duels produced winners and mone-tary bragging rights for a given area, they did not produce,

Richard Tattersall's auction ring began offering fine horses for sale in 1766. Tattersalls continues to auction thoroughbreds today.

at least amongst the sporting public, a horse that could be called a hero, one that would make horse racing a popular sport like baseball or boxing.

Sometime back before the turn of the past century, James Gordon Bennett, seeking readers for his penny newspaper the *New York Herald*, began publishing daily accounts of horse races. Benjamin Day followed in his *New York Sun*, and so, too, did all those while-you-get-your-haircut weeklies of the time, like the *Police Gazette* and *Spirit of the Times*. Together, they brought horse racing to the people. And produced one of the first national sports celebrites in America: a horse named Dan Patch.

Dan Patch was a pacer who made the collective pulse of America race. As a celebrity he outshone them all. At state fairs, Teddy Roosevelt, William Jennings Bryan, and even The Burning of Moscow fireworks display ran poor seconds to this four-legged national monument.

Foaled in 1896, Dan Patch was a gaunt, scraggly colt with knees too knobby, hocks too curved, and legs too long. In short, he had neither the looks nor the temperament of a racer. His owner, Dan Messner, a village storekeeper in Oxford, Indiana, thought so little of his chances that Dan Patch was four years old before he ever competed in a race.

Finally, thinking him nothing more than "a pretty fair delivery horse," Messner was worn down by the importuning of Dan Patch's trainer and entered his horse in a match race against two speedsters of modest reputation around the world of Oxford. The bay colt won in straight heats. Dan Patch never lost a race from that day on.

Seeking to cash in on his prize horse, Messner sold him for $20,000 in 1901. The following year, the new owner multiplied his investment threefold, selling Dan Patch to Marion Willis Savage, a Minneapolis manufacturer. The record amount paid for Dan Patch was mere seed money to create a walking, running, and pacing advertisement for his International Stock Food Company.

From that day forward, wherever and whenever Dan Patch raced—traveling the Midwest and the Southwest in his private railway car—he became the prime attraction at local fairs, his appearance preceded by advance men who papered the countryside with huge signs heralding "Dan Patch. The Wonder Horse." His fame spread. And, with it, the sales of International Stock Food Company.

Soon, local farm publications were filled with ads offering *The Racing Life of Dan Patch* for the price of a one-cent stamp—stock-food literature enclosed free of charge, of course. That was followed by "Genuine Dan Patch horseshoes" at $1 apiece, Dan Patch cigars, Dan Patch sleds, Dan Patch coaster wagons, Dan Patch hobbyhorses, Dan Patch foods, and Dan Patch farm machines. Even a railroad was named in his honor. The horse called by *The Horse Review* "so phenomenal as to defy comparison" was to make more than $1 million in purse monies, and another million from the merchandising of his name. Retired to stud in 1910, Dan Patch still inspired millions of his faithful followers to make pilgrimages to his stable outside Minneapolis to take a peek at this living legend.

During the next few years, the horse-racing scene would change radically. Harness racing, born in the farmlands of the Midwest, soon became the victim of progress as man's best friend became obsoleted by the invention of a machine that went faster, the automobile.

And, by the next decade, as America roared into the Roaring Twenties, dedicated to the pursuit of fast action and glamour, thoroughbred racing had eclipsed the standardbred. And produced its own heroes, most notably Man o' War.

The first thoroughbred to capture the public's imagination was Man o' War, whose personal achievements replaced the natural rivalries of the past. Oh, there may have been great horses before Man o' War—horses like Freeland, Rey el Santa Anita, Boundless, Luke Blackburn, Alan-a-Dale, Miss Woodford, Domino, Colin, Roseben, Sysonby, Look Out, and others—but none could match the horse dubbed "The Mostest" by his groom Will Harbut and "Big Red" by his legion of followers, most of whom would have challenged you if, as someone said, you took his name in vain.

Grantland Rice, the most prominent sportswriter of the day, put into words the feelings of most Man o' War fans when he wrote: "Man o' War was something different—something extra—as great a competitor as Ty Cobb, Jack Dempsey, Tommy Hitchcock, Ben Hogan, or anyone else. He struck me always as one who had a furious desire to win. He started running from the post and he was giving his best at the wire—all the way with all he had."

Starting with Man o' War, the pantheon of all-time horses included, in no particular order, such greats as Exterminator, Lexington, Twenty Grand, Equipoise, Gallant Fox, Seabiscuit, Count Fleet, War Admiral, Sarazen, Johnstown, Citation, Armed, Alsab, Stymie, Assault, Challedon, Noor, Phar Lap, Whirlaway, Omaha, Native Dancer, Tim Tam, Kelso, John Henry, Dr. Fager, Affirmed and Alydar (as a dual entry), Secretariat, Seattle Slew, Cigar, Ruffian, et cetera, etc., etc., etc.—the et ceteras going on for about five pages or more.

And the fans of their day fell in love with each and every, as they had with Man o' War.

It's a love that defies definition, one that sent the entire continent of Australia into mourning when their native son, Phar Lap, died; one that inspired youngsters to write poems and paint watercolors in honor of Kelso; one that prompted members of the press, normally a cynical and crusty crowd, to turn teary-eyed and even dedicate books to their favorites; one that animates owners, jockeys, and fans, and causes them to employ the very word *love* in their appreciation of these four-legged friends.

It's a love that has been celebrated in poetry, art, books, movies, and song, and it is ever present in our pop culture. (For references, what horse lover can hear the "William Tell Overture" and not think of the Lone Ranger and his "great horse" Silver?)

And it's a love that prompted a correspondent of Teddy Roosevelt back in 1907 to write: "God forbid I should go to any heaven in which there are no horses."

With apologies to Mr. Ed, a horse is not *just* a horse, of course, of course. It is something more. Much more. And that is our purpose in bringing you *Horse Sense*.

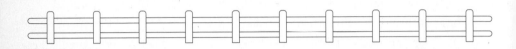

Del Mar racetrack (Copyright © Getty Images, Getty Images North America).

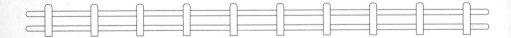

THE TRACKS

The world of horse racing is one with a wide curriculum, as can be expected from the second most widely attended sport in the United States, with a total impact on the U.S. gross domestic product of more than $112 billion annually, according to a 1995 study.

It is a world that goes far beyond the form charts and the betting windows, and includes not only trainers, jockeys, backstretchers, and track employees—who can be seen at the tracks—but also an unknown and unseen world, extending from the breeding farms and horse sales to the tracks themselves, along with unfathomable financial "Equinomics" that make that world go 'round.

What better place to pick up the thread than at the most famous of all sporting events, racing's classic, the Kentucky Derby?

To the rest of the country, the advance signs of spring are the warble of birdies that sing, tra la, the breaking of northern ice floes, the first midwestern tornado, and the visits of geese to local ponds. But in the bluegrass country of Kentucky, there is only one true harbinger of spring: the Kentucky Derby.

Derby time is a gathering of the racing clan, that unchartered but widely known fellowship of owners and breeders. And, in the week before the Derby, they congregate amongst the pink-and-white dogwoods of Lexington to rub elbows with those similarly inclined to come and go, speaking of Canonero and other Derby horses, their stories hardly ending at the three-mile limit, but extending far out to sea.

The mix of owners and breeders is a heady brew, an elite group who wear the cordon bleu colors and can trace their lineage back to earlier, class-ridden times when the likes of August Belmont and William Vanderbilt, born to the industrial purple with wealth so large they looked for outlets, pursued the things they cherished—like golden fleeces, Holy Grails, treasures, crowns, and beautiful horses—and turned racing into a gilt-edged sport.

That elite group, whose bloodlines are as pedigreed as their horses, have taken others onto their sparsely populated island—a diverse group ranging from corporate CEOs to sports moguls to a smattering of monied blue collarites. And no longer is this group merely the Founding Fathers, but Daughters as well. Still, even with the changing of the Old Guard, they remain the caretakers of the sport, the keepers of racing's rich traditions.

The sport of racing flourished in the South as far back as the eighteenth century, and, by the end of the nineteenth, Kentucky and environs—extending into Tennessee and Virginia—had become the center of the thoroughbred industry.

One of the South's leading owners and breeders of the time was General W. G. Harding, only recently returned from what he called "the late unpleasantness" to run Tennessee's Belle Meade Farm, which was home in the late nineteenth century to the likes of Bramble, Enquirer, Luke Blackburn, Great Tom, and Iroquois. Harding attributed his success to "the real blue grass and the pure limestone water that our horses drink and thrive on . . ."

St. Louis sportswriter Al Spink, taking in the sights and sounds of Belle Meade, took pen in hand to describe it in the style of the day:

> Belle Meade lay sleeping in the sun.
> That golden autumn day
> The live oaks wore their scarlet coats
> And breeches lichen gray,
> The beech had changed its green attire
> For dress of brown and gold,
> And blue-grass pastures far away
> In emerald billows rolled.

Even though Kentucky and the surrounding area had gained a reputation for raising the best thoroughbreds, after Louisville's Woodlawn Race Course shuttered its doors in 1870, there was no place to run same. It was at that point that an adventurous soul named Colonel Meriwether Lewis Clark, Jr.—who came by his name honestly, his grandfather having been the Clark of the famed Lewis & Clark Expedition—built a track on eighty acres of land leased from his uncles, John and Henry Churchill. The track, called the Louisville Jockey Club, opened on Monday, May 17, 1875, with four races, the featured race being a mile-and-a-half affair patterned after the famed Epsom Derby and named, for lack of a better title, the Kentucky Derby.

But to call that initial running of the Derby a classic would be overstating its then-importance, there being longer-running races, like the Belmont, the Travers Stakes, and the Preakness, and even more important races on the calendar, such as the American Derby and the Futurity. Then there was the problem of eastern owners considering Louisville little more than a western outpost and, in those travel-challenged days, refusing to ship their horses that far to compete (something owner Sam Riddle declined to do with Man o' War as late as 1920). And then there was the problem that for many years the Derby was not the first of the three races which came to be known as the Triple Crown, with the Preakness, as late as 1930, run first. Whatever the reason, the first running of the Kentucky Derby was considered to be far less than the classic it is today.

Many of the early tracks were tracks in the same way raisins can be considered fruits—technically, and only in a manner of speaking, some being private tracks built on farmland, others mere city streets blocked off for racing. But, by the third quarter of the nineteenth century, ovals resembling modern-day tracks were being built from California to New York, from Kentucky to Maryland, and throughout the Midwest to accommodate Americans who now had the leisure time and money to indulge in such activities as sports—both participating and spectating.

As more and more facilities were built, the ancient upper-class structure began to fall and, in the most rampant form of democracy, the commoner was soon rubbing elbows with the elite. One story about the freemasonry found at racetracks was told by a St. Louis sports editor of the time, who accompanied the then-president of the United States, U. S. Grant, to the old Cote Brillanté race course in St. Louis, where he introduced

Grant to a man identified as "J. J. Edwards," who had an entry in that afternoon's feature race. After shaking hands with "Mr. Edwards," the president walked on and after a few steps turned to the editor and said, "I've seen that man before. It's a face and eyes I have never forgotten . . . I first saw him one day when we were after Quartrell's band. He was the last away. Some said it was Jesse James . . ." Here the president paused and then went on, "But that couldn't be the same man, could it? That name sounds much like Jesse Edward James. But, of course, the two are not related . . ." But they were more than related; they were one and the same.

By the end of the nineteenth century, racetracks were sprouting up all over the map, almost like . . . well, racetracks, although, truth to tell, grouping all under the heading of "racetracks" would be about as apt a description as coupling Pekingese and Great Danes under the same heading, many tracks resembling mere soup tureens. It was a time when they were opening new racecourses every day in St. Louis, when new tracks sprang up in New Orleans, Chicago, San Francisco, New York State, and New Jersey. A boom time for racing.

However, along with the boom in racing came an unwanted companion: gambling, with betting rings dedicated to the shearing of the locals from their coin and valuables accompanying the opening of most of the new tracks.

In Chicago, where racing was held every day, summer and winter, at Garfield Park in the heart of the west side residential district, avarice was exploited in its most naked form, with the gambling ring educating all, housewives included, to the pleasure of betting on the races. It was said that the gamblers were clearing as much as $100,000 a day in turn-of-the-century dollars and that most of those in the area had the wolf glued to their doors like a window decal, with 99 percent of all the furniture in the neighborhood owned by money sharks.

Having gone in with shoestrings and come out with tanneries, the gambling interests, not content with merely providing an asylum for the restless and unwise dollar invested by plucked and singed birds of fortune, now sought control of the entire industry, whether by building new racecourses or buying old.

At a time when Chicago's Garfield Park Race Track was at the height of its prosperity, Ed Corrigan, a member of the professional tipping bureau, came along and, with the Chicago politicians and police in his back pocket, built the Hawthorne Race Course. What ensued was one of the fiercest battles since the days of the Pullman strike, with each side using every artifice within their wiles and power to cripple the other. That failing, they resorted to force. And when, at Corrigan's direction, members of the Chicago constabulary rushed the gates of Garfield in an attempt to close it, they found it protected by Pinkerton men. The result was predictable: violence and bloodshed.

Soon after the Chicago fiasco, Corrigan surfaced as part owner of the Tanforan track in San Francisco. But here, again, he encountered competition, this time from another invader from Chicago, Tom Williams. Denied entry into the city Herb Caen later called "Baghdad by the Bay" by the powers-that-be, Williams became his own power-that-be, setting up shop across the Bay in a town of his own creation, Emeryville, complete with his own mayor and city council which, not surprisingly, enacted laws allowing a racetrack within its corporate limits and any old thing Williams wanted at the track—from craps to foreign books, and from loaded dice to faro, keno, and chuck-a-luck. It was not long before those who frequented Tanforan found that the sunshine and warmth at Emeryville was an odds-on favorite over the blankets of fog and chilly winds they had to endure on the San Francisco side and, with the Emeryville track getting all the play, Tanforan soon became a fog itself. With first Emeryville, then Oakland, and now San Francisco in his control, Corrigan grew even more arrogant, and sought to control all of California's racing.

With similar struggles for control of tracks in New Orleans, New York, and St. Louis between rival gambling interests, small wonder they should arouse the attention of dedicated reformers. For, it was at that point in our social history that the reform movement was on the move, a movement fueled by what H. L. Mencken called "that haunting fear that someone, somewhere, may be happy," feeling that if Dante were alive and living in America at the beginning of the twentieth century, he would have created special circles in hell for anything that smacked of fun, from drinking to wagering, even to women riding bicycles. (A group known as the Watch and Ward Society even campaigned for the banning of the painting *September Morn*, that innocuous painting that adorned White Rock beverage labels and ads of later years, because of its suggestiveness.)

And so, with a clicking of tongues which sounded for all the world like a meeting of the Spanish Castanet Union, the crusaders, in tandem with progressive reform politicians, began to enact laws declaring bookmaking and all kinds of wagering at race tracks a felony.

The first olive out of the legislative jar came in 1908, when New York governor Charles Evans Hughes signed into law the Agnew-Hart Bill, an antiwagering act aimed at the betting rings and, not incidentally, Tammany, which had interests in New York tracks. The next year, California governor Hiram Johnson signed a similar bill, one aimed as much at Emeryville's Tom Williams in particular as at racetrack wagering in general. And on and on it went, as state after state followed the lead of New York and California, like Mary's little lamb, as antiwagering laws swept the country.

Not only did the gambling community wilt away like snails that had just received a handful of salt between the eyes, but so too did the racetracks, which closed all across the country, disappearing like a shadow after the sun goes behind a cloud—leaving racing, as they say in the theater district, "dark." All of a sudden there was no rent to pay, no troubles, no use, and no nothing for racetrack properties worth millions in the morning and which could not be given away by nightfall, the flour and the oat bins in the horses' stalls empty and the tracks equally so.

However, even during this "turf crash," a few isolated oases remained. One of those was the Commonwealth of Kentucky, where, at Churchill Downs, the track's then-vice president, Matt J. Winn, dusted off a few pari-mutuel machines and installed the imports from France, cutting out the gambling ring middlemen with this new form of betting. The machines were to prove to be racing's salvation—and the beginning of Churchill Downs's ascendancy to become, in time, one of the nation's premier tracks.

Over the years, many tracks have crumbled, been destroyed by fire, failed because of mismanagement or political interference, or been bought out or merged out of existence. But others, like Churchill Downs, have managed to survive, even in the face of the antigambling fervor of the early twentieth century. And, when they returned, those old stalwarts, together with new racecourses built after World War I, began introducing newfangled innovations to improve racing and broaden its appeal to postwar fans—including pari-mutuel machines, teletimers, photo-finish cameras, mechanical starting gates, and running races in a counterclockwise manner. All of which proved appealing to its bread-and-bettor—the fans who returned in flocks, like seabirds to the decks of ships after the waters had calmed.

NORTH AMERICAN RACETRACKS

State	Track
Arkansas	Oaklawn Park
Arizona	Flagstaff
	Rillito Park
	Turf Paradise
	Yavapia
California	Bay Meadows Race Course
	Bay Meadows Fair
	Del Mar Thoroughbred Club
	Fairplex Park
	Ferndale
	Fresno
	Golden Gate Fields
	Hollywood Park
	Los Alamitos
	Oak Tree Racing Association
	Pleasanton
	Sacramento
	Santa Anita Park
	Santa Rosa
	Stockton
	Solano
Colorado	Arapahoe Park
Delaware	Delaware Park
Florida	Calder Race Course
	Gulfstream Park
	Hialeah Park
	Ocala Training Center
	Tampa Bay Downs
Idaho	Les Bois Park
	Minidoka County Fair at Rupert

(continued)

(CONTINUED)

State	Track
Illinois	Arlington Park
	Fairmount Park
	Hawthorne Race Course
	Sportsman's Park
Indiana	Hoosier Park
Iowa	Prairie Meadows
Kansas	Anthony Downs
	Eureka Downs
	Woodlands
Kentucky	Churchill Downs
	Ellis Park
	Keeneland Racing Association
	Kentucky Downs
	Turfway Park
Louisiana	Delta Downs
	Evangeline Downs
	Fair Grounds
	Louisiana Downs
Maryland	Laurel Park
	National Steeplechase Association
	Pimlico Race Course
	Timonium
Massachusetts	Great Barrington
	Three County Fair, Northampton
	Suffolk Downs
Michigan	Great Lakes Downs
	Mount Pleasant Meadows
Minnesota	Canterbury Park
Montana	Great Falls
	Yellowstone Downs

(CONTINUED)

State	Track
Nebraska	Atokad Park
	Columbus Races
	Fonner Park
	Horsemen's Park
	Lincoln State Fair
Nevada	Winnemucca (Humboldt County Fair)
New Hampshire	Rockingham Park
New Jersey	Atlantic City
	Meadowlands
	Monmouth Park
New Mexico	Downs at Albuquerque
	Albuquerque State Fair
	Ruidoso Downs
	Santa Fe
	Sunland Park
	Sunray Park
New York	Aqueduct
	Belmont Park
	Finger Lakes
	Saratoga
Ohio	Beulah Park
	River Downs
	Thistledown
Oklahoma	Blue Ribbon Downs
	Fair Meadows, Tulsa
	Remington Park
	Will Rogers Downs
Oregon	Grants Pass
	Salem, Lone Oak
	Portland Meadows

(continued)

(CONTINUED)

State	Track
Pennsylvania	Penn National
	Philadelphia Park
Texas	Gillespie County Fair
	Lone Star Park
	Manor Downs
	Retama Park
	Sam Houston Race Park
Virginia	Colonial Downs
Washington	Emerald Downs
	Harbor Park
	Playfair Race Course
	Sun Downs
West Virginia	Charles Town
	Mountaineer Park
Wyoming	Wyoming Downs

Canada	Track
Alberta	Lethbridge
	Northlands
	Stampede Park
British Columbia	Desert Park
	Hastings Park
	Kam-Loops
	Kin-Park
	Sunflower Downs
Manitoba	Assiniboia Downs
Ontario	Fort Erie
	Woodbine
Saskatchewan	Marquis Downs

As both old and newly built tracks rode racing's postwar wave of popularity, one track began to become synonymous with racing: Churchill Downs. It would be hard, if not impossible, to point to the exact moment when Churchill Downs became *the* most-famous track in America. Some old timers, long ago mowed down by errant trolley cars, would, in their time, have pointed to the year 1902, when Colonel Winn, along with others, took control of the faltering race course and revived its flagging finances and signature race. Others, to 1915, when Harry Payne Whitney shipped his unbeaten filly Regret to Louisville for the forty-first running of the then-lower-cased derby—a race won by Regret, who became the first filly to win the derby—and the only one until Genuine Risk in 1980. Still others, to 1919 when Sir Barton became what is known as the first Triple Crown Winner, although the term was not coined until 1930 by the writer Charles Hatton to describe Gallant Fox, the second horse to sweep the three races now combined under the Triple Crown. (The very use of the phrase in 1919 to describe Sir Barton was a revision somewhat akin to calling the Great War "World War I," as if everyone knew another already had been scheduled.) Some may even suggest that the year 1928 was when the Derby *became* "The Derby," the Derby's fame until that time having floated on the dual wings of print and word of mouth but which, in '28, verbally floated on the words of Clem McCarthy to an audience listening from a continental distance to the first radio broadcast of the Derby on an NBC national hookup. And several others, May 3, 1952, when the Derby first aired on television, and announcer Bill Corum dubbed the race "the Run for the Roses."

Whatever the reason, Churchill Downs and the Kentucky Derby became the most famous twosome in racing, linked together as if they were two wire coat hangers.

And Kentuckians began to proudly tell all who would listen, with the solemnity of Moses relaying the Tablets from the Mount, that there was no place like Churchill Downs, with its famous twin spires and its mint-julepy hospitality. Nonetheless, there was many a track that could rival what, borrowed from Stephen Foster, Kentuckians called their "Old Kentucky Home." However, on Derby Week those other worthies tended to be as overlooked as Whistler's father.

A h! but yes, Virginia—and New York and Illinois and California and all points north, east, west, and south—there are other great tracks throughout the United States, tracks that could be considered Churchill Downs's equal and included in what might be termed racing's top tier, those 152 tracks known, in trackspeak, as the top tier. And each a jewel in its own setting in much the same way as Churchill Downs and its twin spires—from Santa Anita, Del Mar, and Hollywood Park in California to Arlington Park in Illinois; Gulfstream in Florida; and Belmont, Aqueduct, and Saratoga in New York. And, if you were writing footnotes, you could write *ibid* alongside the names of several others as well, each and every a monument to the sport. And almost every track comes with its own cheering section, those fans and followers who will tout (good word, that!) its unique appearances and appurtenances, in much the same way as the cheerleaders of Churchill Downs will theirs.

After all, who among those who have ever attended the all-too-brief summer meet at that wonderful anachronism known as

Saratoga hasn't come away rhapsodizing about the irresistible charm of this tiny town in the foothills of the Adirondacks with its famous Big Red Spring and soft, gentle afternoons under ancient elms? Who at Del Mar doesn't rave about the breathtaking view of the Pacific? And among the attendees at Belmont, called "the Taj Mahal of Racetracks," for obvious reasons beyond its century-old trees and far-more recent plantings, does not come away with an appreciation of why August Belmont II built it as a tribute to the sport? The list of each of those top-tier tracks goes on and on . . . each offering something appetizing above and beyond the main course of the day, racing.

TRACK SIZE			
Track	Location	Size	Type
Saratoga	Main	1 ⅛ Miles	
	Turf	1 Mile	Outer turf
	Steeplechase	⅞ Mile	Inner turf
Belmont	Main course	1 ½ Miles	
	Widner turf	1 ⁵⁄₁₆ Miles	Outer turf
	Inner turf	1 Mile	Inner turf
Aqueduct	Main track	1 ⅛ Miles	
	Inner track	1 Mile	
	Turf course	⅞ Mile	
Churchill Downs	Main course	1 Mile	
	Turf course	⅞ Mile	
Pimlico	Main course	1 ¼ Miles	Incl. chute
	Turf course	⅞ Mile	
Santa Anita	Main course	1 Mile	2 Chutes
	Turf course	⅞ Mile	

Data source: Equibase/Daily Racing Form.

Just as there are several different settings for tracks, so too are there several different configurations. For tracks are hardly partial to a single orthodoxy, the very word *oval*, as in oval tracks, an elastic one, admitting to paper clip-shaped and hairpin-shaped turns (Pimlico), sweeping, massive turns on a track so large its area code changes twice during a race (Belmont), long and loooooonger straightaways (New Orleans Fair Grounds) and starting chutes (Santa Anita). It's almost as if each track—top tier or no—takes pride in its own track configuration as well as its setting.

But over and above the differences in track configurations, surfaces also differ from track to track. California, for instance, with more tracks than any other state—twelve—has a preponderance of what Grantland Rice called "dynamite" tracks, with faster times registered than those of their Eastern counterparts. The reason for these dynamite tracks is that primitive liquid known as water, a rare commodity in parts of California. (Remember the movie *Chinatown*, in which Jack Nicholson utters the line "All this just for fuckin' water?" to describe a battle over water rights?) Rather than watering their tracks, California racecourse owners merely keep them dry and hard instead of damp and manicured, in turn giving us sprinters like Swaps and Dr. Fager.

With apologies to George Orwell, all tracks are not created equal, either in their setting, their track configuration, their surface, or their grade. And assuredly not in their purse structure.

The difference between a top-tier track and one that isn't might, at times, be as plain as the egg on the chin of a hungry diner patron. Other times, it isn't.

A quick wet-your-finger-and-hold-it-in-the-air measure might be the amount of the purses dispersed by a track. For, in that world of higher horse finance—call it *Equinomics*, if you will—the track offering purses in the neighborhood of $300,000 for a nine-to-twelve race card is more oft than not a top-level track compared to one offering a "mere" $100,000 per card.

A more widely accepted measure of a top-tier rating is that of a track playing host to a race graded as one of the classics, as determined by the Thoroughbred Owners and Breeders Association (TOBA), a group consisting of TOBA trustees, track officials, and editors of *The Blood-Horse* magazine. Thus, we have the classic tier, or tier one of three distinct tiers, which includes Aqueduct, Belmont, and Saratoga in New York; Churchill Downs and Keeneland in Kentucky; Hollywood Park, Santa Anita, and Del Mar in California; Pimlico and Laurel in Maryland; Gulfstream and Calder in Florida; and Arlington Park in Illinois. The second of the three tiers consists of forty-two tracks, regional in nature, which are the backbone of American racing. The third tier, predominately seasonal in nature, is basically the county fair circuit.

If, as has been said, money is the root of all evil, then the biggest rooters are the owners and trainers who, in a case of show us the money, follow the green breadcrumbs straight to those tracks offering it. Bottom line, purses are racing's financial roundelay, with tracks offering larger and larger purses in the hopes of attracting the best horses available, owners and trainers taking their horses to where the most money is offered, and fans and bettors coming out to follow the best horses available. Put it altogether and it spells "m-o-n-e-y."

The *purse*—a term derived from the olde English custom of tethering an actual purse containing the winning amount to a pole marking the finish line where the winning jockey crossing the line grabbed it as he passed—is today defined as "the total money awarded in a race." Such a definition is about as complete a description as defining Noah Webster as a "writer."

As far as can be determined by racing historians, one of the first purses in America goes back to 1851, when, in the first organized thoroughbred race in California history, San Franciscans ponied up $250 as a purse for a three-horse sweepstakes—then the full handle for *stakes*—at San Francisco's Pioneer Course.

Yet, back in those early days out west, when men were men and women were damned glad of it, it was not unusual for owners to race their horses for prizes, not purses, as Don Juan Sepulveda of California's San Gabriel Valley did in 1857. Sepulveda, who had an unbeaten horse by the same name, challenged one and all to run against his horse for 10,000 head of cattle, an offer later amended to either the cattle or their equivalent in coin, $200,000. Two years after the offer was issued, the Treat brothers of San Francisco took Señor Sepulveda up on his offer and, with an imported Andalusian horse named Black Swan, won cattle and coin.

By the end of the nineteenth century, such challenges for prizes had become part of history. And, by the beginning of the new century, a purse structure as we know it today, one based solely on coin of the realm, had replaced it, with an average purse of almost $1,000. But, after the enactment of the antigambling laws, the average dropped by almost two-thirds and didn't reverse its downward trend until the antigambling laws were taken off the books and World War I had ended. The 1920 Kentucky Derby set the pace with a record winner's purse of $30,375.

Throughout the Roaring Twenties, purses continued to roar as well, with total purse monies reaching the $10 million mark in 1924, and 1929 Futurity victor Whichone winning a record purse of $105,370.

Even though total purse monies reached $13 million in 1931, the Depression began to erode the purse structure as it did everything else. With tracks cutting back on their purses—Agua Caliente awarding Phar Lap only half of its advertised $100,000 purse in '32 and the Derby reducing its purse from $50,000 to $30,000 in '34—by the depths of the Depression, purses totaled only $8.5 million, barely two-thirds of what they had been just three years earlier.

As the economy recovered, so too did racing's purse structure. Aided and abetted by the openings of several new tracks in the '30s—like Del Mar, Hollywood Park, and Hialeah—purses soared upward, reaching a total of $16 mil by 1940. Then, when peace broke out in 1945—just in time to preserve the runnings of the Triple Crown classics that year—purses began to skyrocket, topping first $100 mil, then $200, then $400, $800, and, by 2001, over $1 billion, an average increase of 4.38 percent annually for the previous decade. It got so that Willie Shoemaker, who had retired in the early 1990s, could only wistfully look at the purses one decade later and say, "I'd have been a godzillionaire if I had been racing today instead of when I did."

All Derby Week long, the racing community makes its way to Louisville—owners, trainers, media, and fans, both privileged and working class alike—for racing's showcase, the Kentucky Derby. Some make the pilgrimage just for the race itself; others to

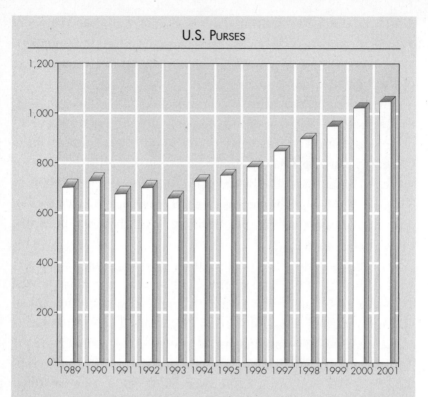

U.S. PURSES

National purses are a leading economic indicator of the health of racing. Although U.S. purses continued their ascent in 2001, the rate of growth slowed to 3.6 percent, with the bulk of the increase derived from two states. In New Jersey, purses were boosted by a one-time $11.7 million subsidy from the state legislature, while in West Virginia, purses increased $21.6 million due in large part to continued expansion of VLT (video lottery terminal) operations at the state's tracks. *Source:* Copyright © The Jockey Club. All rights reserved.

enjoy the weeklong activities and racing at Churchill Downs. It's a week where, as Red Smith said, "Tips go from bellhop to tourist instead of vice versa."

For those choosing to attend the week of races, it's almost racing's version of spring training, a chance for everyone to take pencils out of mothballs and do a little figuring in the margins of their programs and scan their *Racing Forms* as they handicap the many races before the Derby—the maidens, claimers, the handicaps, and other stakes races—and listen to winter stories, all in the name of getting ready for the BIG one.

Each of the races offered by Churchill Downs that week is, like those of all tracks everywhere, determined by the track's racing secretary who, for every meet, is responsible for publishing the exact number of races that will be conducted, the type of race, and the purse. And each race for every day of the meet is listed in what is called *The Condition Book*, a book published well in advance of the start of the meet that contains the schedule of different events, and allows for trainers and owners to prepare for those in which they would like their horses to compete.

Chief among those events are thoroughbred racing's largest component, the claiming race, which accounts for 49 percent of all races. When you add the subcategory maiden races, that percentage climbs to over 65 percent.

The condition of entry for a *claiming race*, a race dating back to England in the seventeenth century, when such races were called *selling races*, is that horses entered into a claimer are entered for sale, the owners willing to risk losing these not-to-class runners at the price of sale specified before the race by the owner. Say the race is a $50,000 claimer and the owner puts a $40,000 value on his horse, that horse is claimable for $40,000. No more, no less by those having the money on deposit at the track to enter a claim. And, if only one person puts in a claim, then he gets the horse. However, if more than one does, the matter is referred to a little cylindrical box with dice, each claimant given a number by the racing secretary with the claimant whose number comes up getting the horse the second the starting gate springs open. But that's all he gets, not the purse if the claimed horse wins. That belongs to the original owner.

But here a caveat in what might be a chorus in George Gershwin's "It Ain't Necessarily So," which may seem obvious but isn't always: A trainer may have taken a horse and dropped him two classes to enter his horse in a cheaper claiming race with horses he may already have beaten, whether it be for a quick payout or a chance to test his horse in live race conditions after changing his style of running. Or merely to get in another race because the ones he wanted to run his horse in were oversubscribed.

Also, prospective owners might not put in a claim on a horse, assuming that the horse has been entered in a cheaper claiming race because there is something wrong with the horse and the owner merely wants to unload him (or her). Or, it could be that prospective owners hesitate to put in a claim believing the horse to be no bargain, either because the horse is not running in his correct class or because there is no added value to the purchase.

One of the grandmasters of the game is trainer Frank "Pancho" Martin, who has been known to take a cheap claimer, run him in three classes, then have him claimed and subsequently reclaim

Arlington Park hosts the Breeders' Cup 2002. High Chapparal and jockey Michael Kinane captured the victory on the turf (*Getty Images, Getty Images North America*).

him on the downside after the horse had been returned to his correct class. Martin once entered a horse in a $10,000 distance claiming race on a Saturday and, finishing third, collected $1,000 in purse money, then ran the horse again seven days later in a $7,500 claiming race of six furlongs and won, collecting $4,200. When asked by some dandruff scratcher in the writing dodge why he had done what he did, Martin answered, "Look at the numbers . . . if I put him in a $15,000 claimer where he belonged, he might have finished second for $3,000 in purse money and the owner probably would have him claimed for $15,000. This way, the owner got $5,200, kept his horse and we now know he is a better sprinter than a distance horse."

(Here it must be noted that normally purse distribution follows a 60-20-11-9 percent breakdown, with 60 percent going to the winner of the race, 20 percent to the place or second-place horse, 11 percent to the show or third-place horse, and the remaining 9 percent divided between the fourth- and fifth-place finishers—that 10 percent divided between fourth and fifth in different ways, depending upon the track. However, all purse structures varying from track to track, some paying off only on the first three finishers, some on one-through-four and others, one-through-five, depending upon their published schedule.)

The claiming game is a chancy one, with as many winners and losers as can be found at the $2 window. On the upside, Hall of Fame trainer Hirsch Jacobs claimed a two-year-old named Stymie in 1943, the same Stymie who went on to become the world's leading money winner by the end of '47. Conversely, ultimate Derby winner Charismatic went unclaimed in an earlier $62,500 claiming race, those in the know feeling the price was too much to bank on. Little wonder sportswriter Mike Lee called claimers Russian roulette.

Even though the claiming game is a rough-and-tumble one, there are a couple of unwritten rules that are generally followed, even by the most cunning: first, never enter a sick horse in a claiming race; and second, never put a claim in on a person's last horse in the barn.

Maiden races, the second-largest segment of races held in North America, combine both maiden and maiden-claiming races. They are those races in which the horses entered have not won a race.

In theory, a maiden is an untested horse, one who may be placed in this type of race merely to establish its class. But, in reality, it is the level at which every horse naturally starts his or her voyage, Columbus-like, into a new world, but not one where the owner hopes he or she finishes. Sometimes, though, it is, as witnessed by the king of the maidens, Zippy Chippy, an eleven-year-old gelding who is 0-for-93 and counting. Still, before assuming that a horse who has problems breaking his or her maiden is a failure, we refer you to the Hall of Fame section headed Triple Crown Winners, where the first name listed is that of Sir Barton, the 1919 winner, who went 0-for-6 before he figured out that the name of the game was to finish ahead of the other horses in the field.

Allowance races, those races filling the void between claimers and stake races, make up approximately 14 percent of all races held. In a manner similar to that employed in claiming events, the racing secretary drafts certain conditions for allowances, taking into account the number of prior races won within a given period of time, the amount of the purses won in those races and, in some instances, the distance run in those races.

Oftimes, the allowance race is one in which a trainer will race a stakes winner returning after a long layoff or as a tune-up for a stakes race. Such was the case with a two-year-old named Lawrin back in 1937. During his early career he had finished second in six allowances at six different tracks. The next year, as a three-year-old and overcoming a bout with seconditis, he won the Kentucky Derby.

Sometimes, an allowance race graduates to the ranks of a stakes race, as did the forerunner at Keeneland and the $325,000 Grade II Coolmore-Lexington Stakes, which began as the Lexington, originally contested by two-year-olds for a $200,000 purse.

Stakes races go back through the fogbanks of time, to 1831 when the first stakes race, the Phoenix Stakes, was run at the Kentucky Association Track in Lexington, followed by such early stakes races as the McGowen Stakes, the Queens Plate, and the Jerome Handicap—all of which, in a sense, were expansions of the old my-best-can-beat-your-best match races of yore.

Today at last count, there are more than 1,700 stakes races run in North America, some 4 percent of the total number of races, but accounting for more than 21 percent of the $1.2 billion purse structure, making them the very top of racing's money mountain. And the most prestigious as well.

In order to attract the best horses available, tracks must make the purse value of the stakes race significant enough to induce the owners to enter their horses. The normal high calculus of building purses, where the race was not invitational, normally combines subscription fees or money paid by the owners who would like their horses to be considered for the race together with nominating fees paid by the owner to guarantee their horse will be chosen to run, and with entry box fees paid by the owner so their horses will be eligible for the race. Here an asterisk normally reserved for late-arriving trains on schedules: Because each of these scheduled stages are time-sensitive, the purse is frequently augmented by supplemental or penalty fees over and above the normal entry fees paid by the owners of a late-entering horse. Such was the case when the owners of Tiznow decided late in the game to enter their horse in the 2000 Breeders' Cup Classic. Not having paid the required entry fees, amounting to $80,500, they had to pony up a total of $360,000 for their late decision, that money, over and above the $80,500, added to the purse guarantee. The gamble paid off hansomely when Tiznow won the race and a tidy sum of $4,296,000 to boot.

Still, when all these fees, including penalties, are ante'd up, they normally cover only about one-half of the purse value, sometimes leaving tracks to look to sponsors to underwrite the remaining costs. (And, if successful, to name the race after them.) If not, then the track puts up what is called *money added* to supplement the purse.

The 1,700 stakes come in more forms than Baskin-Robbins has flavors, with stake races for two-year-olds, three-year-olds, four-year-olds, five-year-olds, six-year-olds, and up, weight-for-age handicaps, fillies, and just about any variation on the theme imaginable. They include those run in the spotlight for millions of dollars to those lesser ones run in relative obscurity for mere thousands.

The highest quality and most prestigious stakes races are graded by the American Graded Stakes Committee of TOBA, which, taking into consideration several factors such as the race's influence on other races and/or championships and the quality of previous races and their winners, grades the stakes Grade I through Grade III. Those Graded I include such races as the Triple Crown races and the Suburban Handicap at Belmont; Grade II includes the Oaklawn Handicap at Oaklawn Park and the Beverly Hills Handicap at Hollywood Park; and Grade III, among its many races, includes the Philip H. Iselin Handicap at Monmouth Park and the San Bernardino Handicap at Santa Anita. All of which leaves several stakes races ungraded in the eyes of the TOBA committee.

The list of stakes races, graded and ungraded, includes several named after somebody or something-or-other, many to honor those who have contributed to the sport, be they owners, jocks, trainers, or horses, and equally as many just to come up with a name, almost like the college bowl games where almost every one is preceded by some product name that sounds like the "Only-10¢-a-Minute-Long-Distance" Bowl.

The bookkeeper's mind rattles at the sheer number of stake races. There are those named for trainers (Charles Whittingham, Hollywood Park; Ben Jones, Charles Town; and Hirsch Jacobs, Pimlico); for jockeys (Isaac Murphy, Arlington Park; John Longden, Hastings Park; and William "Bill" Hartack, Charles Town); for horses (hundreds, including Man o' War, Belmont; Secretariat, Arlington Park; and Sir Barton, Pimlico); for writers (Damon Runyon, Aqueduct; Jim Murray, Hollywood Park; and Red Smith, Aqueduct); for products (Budweiser, Rillito Park; Subway Sandwiches, Lethbridge; and CJ's Oilfield Services, Grand Prairie); for movies (Ben Hur, Delaware Park; My Fair

Lady, Suffolk Downs; and Snow White, Charles Town); for movie stars (Pat O'Brien and Bing Crosby, Del Mar; Donna Reed and John Wayne, Prairie Meadows); for songs (Lawdy Miss Clawdy, Sportsman's Park; Georgia On My Mind, Calder; and Yellow Brick Road, Charles Town); for historical figures (Thomas Edison, Meadowlands; General Douglas MacArthur, Belmont; and Jean Lafitte, Delta Downs); for sports figures (Bob Feller, Prairie Meadows; Steve Van Buren, Philadelphia Park; and the Baltimore Ravens, Pimilico); and more for names which sound like they were pulled out of a hat (Send More Money, Penn National; Naked Greed, Calder; and Hangover, Hawthorne).

Then there are those races called, for lack of a better name, "overnight stakes," which find their way onto the card after the racing secretary establishes the schedule and meets with the marketing department to develop special stake races—which can run the gamut from companies sponsoring a race to couples celebrating everything and anything from their fifthieth wedding anniversary to their child's Bar Mitzvah. These McStakes, which probably should go under the heading of Name That Race or What to Give Someone Who Has Everything, have given the racing world such stake races as The Boss, held at Tampa Bay Downs in honor of Yankee owner George Steinbrenner (although Boston Red Sox fans might want to change the name, spelling it backward as "The Double S-O-B").

The last category of races is the handicaps, accounting for just 1 percent of all races run. The object of a handicap race is to adjust the weights of each horse so that, theoretically, all finish in a dead heat.

The handicap is the most difficult of all races, requiring a skilled handicapper and a seasoned racing secretary who assign given weights to all the horses in the field based on certain criteria (age, sex, races won, competition, last race won, etc.) to insure parity.

Nevertheless, there are times when it seems as if the weights were plucked out of thin air. If, as the old track adage goes, "weight will stop a freight train," how to explain why Forego carried as much as 135 when he won the Woodward Stakes four years in a row, from 1974 to '77, while Cigar, winning in 1995 and '96, carried only 126 both times? Even so, high weight or no, the great horse Exterminator—of whom his trainer said, "I expect he is one of the dumbest horses I ever saw. He don't know the difference between 115 and 135 pounds"—could win lugging a piano and its player on his back. Or so it was said.

And so, as the races—claimers, maidens, allowances, handicaps, and stakes—wound down on the days before the first Saturday in May and the last echo inside Churchill Downs finally died down, everyone turned their attention to the one that really, really mattered, the big one: the Kentucky Derby.

The late Prince Ahmed bin Salman leading Belmont Stakes winner Point Given, ridden by jockey Gary Stevens *(Copyright © Getty Images, Getty Images North America).*

2

THE OWNERS

On the first Saturday of May, Churchill Downs is, at one and the same time, a patch of land and a state of emotion. For this is Kentucky's annual rite of spring, the Kentucky Derby, a day when, if God wasn't in His heaven and all right with the world, those conditions would prevail as near as possible for America's most famous race.

On the ground level, one could find gaily plumed birds wearing wide-brimmed hats and clothing that would reduce Joseph's coat to a monochrome, mingling with the crowd and making many delightful acquaintances, some of whom they might even remember the next morning. And, at every concession stand, lines that looked like they went all the way from Lou-ie-ville (as they pronounce it down thar) to Cincinnati waiting in anticipation of purchasing souvenir glasses containing something that passed for mint juleps, soon to be deposited either into stomachs or nearby trash receptacles. (As racing's laureate Joe Palmer wrote about juleps: "One's plenty, two's too many, and three ain't half enough.")

Out in the infield, taking part in one of the most riotous celebrations since those of the French Revolution, thousands of casual fans could be seen, mostly those who would drive 5,000 miles just to have their pictures taken standing in front of their own automobiles, there to enjoy the occasion rather than the event, all soaking up the sunshine and whatever else they might find.

And, up in the owners' boxes, called "Millionaires' Row," with a couple of Bs thrown in for good measure, where the popping of corks and the glitter of coin were the scheduled order of the day, maintaining a polite fiction of the goings-on around them, were the monied mileu, the owners. For any and all discussion about the so-called players of the sport must begin with the owners; they are the powers-that-be and the font of all money that underwrites the sport.

Going back to earlier class-ridden times, when the owners of horses were the grandees and noblemen of society, so, too, were the caliphs and captains of early American industry, their names ringing with the sound of money, the once-titled nobility of early racing. Had their tastes been such, they could have ridden in golden chariots; but horses were their passion, and so these members of the early ownership class—aristocrats such as Pierre Lorillard and August Belmont—became, along with more than a few bourbon-and-branch barons, racing's Founding Fathers.

Unfortunately, down through the years, the names of many early-time owners, like the flame of a blown-out candle barely leaving a trace of smoke, have come and gone with little more than a trace, their names lost to memory—like those of E. J. "Lucky" Baldwin and Otto Stiffel and the Dwyer brothers. And when they are remembered at all, remembered only because some stakes race is named in their honor.

Still, even back then, when horses were horses and automobiles unheard of, the elite—for whom money was never the primary consideration of ownership, but did hold a certain fascination—were joined by outsiders, those who bought their way into their select company, including, but hardly limited to, the Dwyer brothers, New York butchers; Dick Croker, a Tammany politician; and several former owners of gambling syndicates who left their gambling rings outside the track and entered the owners' inner circle.

One of the first of those outsiders was William Crockford, a nineteenth-century fishmonger whose gambling successes enabled him to found a gambling house that bore his name and who, in turn, became an owner. A story which has been passed down by those with cauliflower tongues from days of yore has it that Crockford, whose horse Ratan was the favorite for the 1844 "Darby," became so distressed after it was discovered that his horse had been poisoned that he succumbed to a fatal fit of apoplexy. His death left his gambling friends in a dilemma, inasmuch as Crockford also had a heavily backed filly entered in a race run at the same Epsom meet as the Derby. Knowing that news of Crockford having gone to that great stable in the sky would mean the disqualification of the filly, his friends propped up Crockford's body in a window of his house at Epsom, overlooking the racecourse, clearly visible to all, to counteract any rumors of his demise. And the filly won, paying off her backers, before their artifice was discovered.

A more recent example of ownership making, if you'll pardon the expression, strange bedfellows occurred a few years ago

when one of our acquaintances wandered into the enclosed owners' box at the New Orleans Fair Grounds. And what to his won-
dering eyes should appear but the still well-put-together form of
one of the most infamous madams in the French Quarter, looking
for all the world as if she had just stepped out of the pages of
Vogue. Despite the fact that the lace and spun-silk veil in front of
her bonnet partially covered her face, she was still recognizable.
Acknowledging her nod, our acquaintance uttered a few sounds
that made a fair stagger at arranging themselves into something
that sounded like "Here on business or pleasure?" Without blush-
ing, like red wine at the certificate of purity on its label, she answered, "My business is always my pleasure . . ." She then went on,
"I'm in the horse business now. When I sold my business to a gentleman from South America, as a sweetener he threw in two thoroughbreds. I changed my name, and since that day, I have been in
the horse business, and now I own twenty outright and another
seven or so in, shall I say, limited partnerships."

The untitled ruling class of racing, like the Brahmin caste of
old New England, has always looked askance at such outsiders.
Not that they view them as something along the order of widow-
and-orphan oppressors with a touch of Bright's disease thrown in,
mind you, but are wary of admitting mere heirs apparent into
their sport, the Sport of Kings.

Gaining admission to their exclusive club is more difficult
than opening an oyster without a knife. Sure, over the years some
one-time outsiders have been admitted to full fellowship into the
inner circle, but only after they have entered the winner's circle,
as the Taylors did with Seattle Slew and the late Prince Ahmed
bin Salman with War Emblem. Even then, while they gained admission, they only sometimes gained acceptance.

For the racing establishment is a family, one built over long
years, almost going back to the Great Flood, its membership
made up of equal parts blueblood and bluegrass. Its members
proudly point to some of the First Families of Racing, like the

Whitney-Paysons, the Phipps-Millses, the Hancocks, and several others as the true keepers of racing's flame.

However, unlike what Sandburg called "the Family of Man," these First Families are today anything but, being almost equally the families of men *and* women. Going back almost to the turn of the last century when the original owner of the woman's copyright, Mrs. Helen Hay Whitney, founded Greentree Stables, followed by Mrs. Henry Carnegie Phipps's Wheatley Stable in the '20s, the close-knit family no longer was just a fraternity, but open to women who have since become an integral part of the ownership family, investing it with their presence and their winning ways.

And, despite some members of the old guard sniffing that women were in racing only because they love parties, and inherited it, or their husbands gave it to them, nothing could be farther from the truth. Their accomplishments not only comprise a major part of *Who's Who in Racing*, but almost a complete volume. A quick run-though of the pages will tell you of their achievements, from Mrs. Payne Whitney winning two Derbys (with Twenty Grand in 1931 and Shut Out in '42); Mrs. Ethel Mars, of Milky Way Stables; Mrs. Fannie Hertz (who gained instant fame with her quip about Bourbon, Kentucky, where her Stoner Creek Farm was located, saying, "Bourbon is known for fast horses, smooth whiskey, and slow revenoorers"), with two Derby winners (Reigh Count in 1928 and Count Fleet in '43); Mrs. Lucille Wright Markey of Calumet Farms, winner of eight Derbys and two Triple Crown winners (Whirlaway, 1941 and Citation, '48); Florence Graham (better known as Elizabeth Arden, aka "Lady Lipstick"), owner of Maine Chance Farm and of Jet Pilot, the 1947 Derby winner; Mrs. Joan Whitney Payson, co-owner of Greentree Stud and Stage Door Johnny and Tom Fool; Penny Chenery, owner of what Dick Schaap called "The most famous stablemates since Joseph and Mary," Secretariat and Riva Ridge; and Karen Taylor, owner of Seattle Slew, the last two parts of the greatest era of women owners in racing history, the 1970s. The list of legendary women owners could go on and on, including others who have contributed to the rich tradition of racing and given their male counterparts a run for their money, both literally and figuratively.

Bottom line, that's what the racing establishment is all about: tradition. And, not incidentally, money.

In a take-off on F. Scott Fitzgerald's famous line—"Let me tell you about the very rich. They are different from you and me" (to which Ernest Hemingway is reputed to have retorted, "Yes, they have more money")—Ken England, describing the owner-ship class, said, "Horse ownership is the only currency that distin-guishes the truly wealthy from the rest of us."

Money has made some of the strangest associations since Pro-fessor Rorschach first toppled over his inkwell. And on that first Saturday in May, up in Millionaires' Row at Churchill Downs, the owners of the Derby entrants are spending the early part of the afternoon intermingling with a catalogue of constituents along for the ride, other owners, breeders, and friends—along with more than a few friends of friends, standing on the periphery of the goings-on like flies in coffee, attracting attention but hardly enjoying it.

GREAT RACING FARMS
THE MILLIONAIRE CLUB

Stable	Owners
Bohemia Stable	Allaire DuPont
Brookmeade Farm	Isabel Dodge Sloane
Brookside Farm	Madeleine and Allen Paulson
Calumet Farm	Warren Wright Lucille Wright Markey Henryk deKwiatkowski
Christiana Stable	H. W. Lunger
Claiborne Farm	A. B. Hancock
Darby Dab Farm	John W. Galbreath
Elmendorf Farm	Max Gluck Jack Kent Cooke
Fox Catcher Farm	William DuPont, Jr.
Glenn Ridge Farm	Samuel Riddle
Godolphin	Sheikh Mohammed bin Rashid al Maktoum
Golden Eagle Farm	Betty and John Maybee
Greentree Stable	Whitney family
Harbor View Farm	Louis and Patrice Wolfson
Hobeau Farm	Jack Dreyfus
Idle Hour Stock Farm	E. R. Bradley
Juddmonte Farm	Khalid Abdullah
Keeneland Stud Farm	J. O. Keene
King Ranch	Robert J. Kleberg

(continued)

(CONTINUED)	
Stable	Owners
Kinsman Stud Farm	George Steinbrenner
Lane's End	William S. Farish
Lazy F Ranch	Mrs. Martha Farish
Live Oak Plantation	Mrs. Charlotte Webber
Llangollen Farm	Mrs. M. E. Lunn
Loblolly Stable	John E. Anthony
Maine Chance Farm	Elizabeth Arden Graham
Meadow Stable	C. T. Chennery
Milky Way Farm	Ethel V. Mars
Overbrook Farm	W. T. Young
Payson Stud	Virginia Kraft Payson
Pin Oak	Josephine Abercrombe
Rokeby Stable	Paul Mellon
Sagamore Farm	Vanderbilt family
Sam-Son Farm	Ernie Samuel Liza Samuel Tammy Samuel-Balaz
Stone Farm	Arthur B. Hancock III
Stronach Stable	Frank Stronach
Taylor Made Farm	Joe Taylor
Thoroughbred Corporation	Prince Ahmed bin Salman
Wheatley Stable	Mrs. Henry Carnegie Phipps

Source: Daily Racing Form.

For racing is monstrous quicksand, its particles changing rapidly. And nowhere is that more evident than in the buildup to the Derby, as some of the most well-unknown two-year-olds race first in the Futurities, then graduate to that interminable series of races for three-year-old potential Derby horses called "preps," which serve merely as throat-clearings for the Derby and are a survivor sport in and of themselves, the road to the Derby is littered with hopes and hopefuls. Several horses that had been made early favorites for the Derby by those with Delphic franchises having failed to acquit their advance press notices and already fallen by the wayside, while some who had survived the grueling schedule of preps had come up lame, and worse, and been scratched from contention.

And so it was, in a manner not unlike that of church bingo where "winners must be present," that circumstances had arranged themselves so that those few owners up in Millionaires' Row stood alone on the brink of becoming the owner of a Derby winner.

With manners overcharged with courtesy, the owners of Derby entrants now mixed with other owners, telling stop-me-if-you've-heard-this-one-before stories and, in the most felicitous good-luck phrases imaginable, putting the best possible faces on other owners' chances. All the while keeping their fingers crossed for theirs, hoping against hope that Lady Fate would take their charge up in the folds of her skirt and carry it across the finish line first, thereby earning them everlasting fame as a Derby winner and becoming a member of racing's elite.

The door to entering the ranks of racing's elite ownership class isn't one that needs a key but instead just the right combination of timing and, more importantly, money.

One who tried to buy his way in on a grand scale was Washington Redskins owner Jack Kent Cooke, who, when challenged by fellow NFL owner Eugene Klein to "come in, the water's fine," went out and bought Elmendorf Farm in 1984 from the estate of Max Gluck for $43 million, a then king's ransom, to buy into the Sport of Kings. The purchase not only brought a bump to his wallet but a lump to his throat as Cooke trumpeted, "With this purchase, I should be able to beat Klein to the Derby winner's circle."

While others, like Richard Croker who bought part of General W. G. Harding's Belle Meade Farm back in the previous century, had fared very well indeed, thank you!, such was not the case with Cooke. His famous Midas touch, which had once made so many of the things he touched golden, now deserted him in the tough and unpredictable racing business. Elmendorf proved not only a financial disappointment, but a blow to his ego as well: Klein beat him to the Derby winner's circle with Winning Colors in 1988, while the best Cooke's horses could do was finish twelfth. Spitting out the bit, Cooke put Elmendorf back on the market for $7.5 mil, not including horses, just before he bought the farm himself in '97.

But one need not buy farms—lock, livestock, and barrel—to enter the realm of ownership. The easiest way of entering is at the claiming level, where 30 percent of today's leading owners started. It may not be as sexy as buying at auctions but, then again, Seabiscuit was once relegated to the claiming ranks. And trainer Hirsch Jacobs claimed two-year-old Stymie, who would go on to become the then leading money winner, for $1,500 in 1943. And it certainly isn't as expensive, not taking the riches only a poobah from a Persian Gulf sultanate can muster from the loose change rattling around in his pocket. Even Prince Ahmed bin Salman, owner of War Emblem, started modestly, with a string of claiming horses.

A second way to become an owner is by buying horses at private sales. Here a caveat: This is a world that traces its ancestry to the horse traders of old, where bending the truth is part and parcel of the deal, where anything goes and buyer beware. And down through the more than a few sellers revert to their natural roots.

They used to tell the story of "Ole Kentuck" where a prospective buyer, looking over a horse for sale and finding nothing wrong with him, asked the owner, "How come you want to sell him?" As the story goes, the owner replied, "He's a showoff . . . When they play a fanfare, he dances. He even whinnies to music. And when they take his picture after a win, he turns his head so's it's a profile shot." To which the buyer said, "Those antics could be cute, I'll buy him." As the vendor took his money, he shouted to the horse, "Okay, Tomboy, get up and do your 'lame' impression."

Another age-old story has it that a prospective buyer asked the owner to name his price for the horse he was selling, to which the owner named $1,000. The buyer countered with an offer of $100, and the owner accepted, saying, "That's a helluva discount, but I'll take it." As the buyer counted out his money, he couldn't resist asking the seller why he had accepted $100 after first offering the horse for ten times the amount. "Well," the seller drawled, "I thought mabee you'd like to own a thousand-dollar horse."

More recently, Cotton "Cot" Campbell of Georgia's Dogwood Stable told a story on himself of the time he had a selection sale for some of the neighboring monied Atlantans interested in owning horses. On the first day of the sale, his exercise boy, aboard one of the horses, took him for a two- to three-furlong ride and then, trotting by Campbell and the money in concert assembled, let out a whoop and hollered, "Oh, whee, Mr. Campbell, I never been on a horse that fast." And, just as fast, the monied laid down their wine and cheese and reached for their pens and checkbooks ready to purchase a horse which, in Campbell's words, "couldn't outrun a fat man."

Just as Campbell's "salesmanship" is a throwback to the old horse traders of yore, their methods were undoubtedly an extension of those employed by an early-seventeenth-century carrier named Thomas Hobson, who, when customers came into his stables to hire a horse, were given a choice of either taking the horse nearest the door or none at all, to ensure that each customer had an equal chance of hiring a good or bad horse and that each horse had an equal chance of receiving good or bad treatment by its handler. Hence the term "Hobson's choice."

Stories of sales shenanigans abound. Jimmy Breslin tells the story of a legendary Kentucky horse dealer named Colonel Phil Chinn, who played every angle known to the world of horse dealing, even sometimes borrowing farms to impress buyers. During workouts at Keeneland, he would, according to Breslin, move in the eighth pole, previously affixed to a tree, so that his for-sale horses were clocked at faster times than they had actually run. One day, a University of Kentucky professor, given to taking in the sun while watching the workouts, looked first at the pole, then at the tree, and audibly said to one and all, "They moved the tree!" To which Chinn shouted, "God damn it, shut up!"

However, such stories are few and far between, like fruit suspended in aspic. For the most part, even though there are a handful of examples where buyers have mistaken the seller's huffery and puffery for the truth and been referred to A. Lincoln's sonnet, "You can fool some of the people . . ." all it requires is a little old-fashioned horse sense to find the right horse at the right price, or better, at private sales.

There are far more feel-good stores in the private sale sector than cautionary tales, the most famous one being the purchase, just weeks before the 2002 Kentucky Derby, of 90 percent of Derby winner War Emblem by Prince Ahmed bin Salman from Chicago businessman Russell Reineman for $900,000.

On a smaller scale, there was the time a few years back when Allen Paulson found his farm overstocked and, in an effort to reduce the number of horses on the farm, decided to unload some. One of those who came a-calling was trainer Sonny Hine who, fancying one, asked its price and condition. Told by Paulson its price was $25,000 and that it was in "good shape," Hine accepted the deal subject to the horse being vetted, even *hondling* the price down in the bargain. However, when the veterinarian checked the horse he found a bone chip in the horse's ankle, and Hine rescinded his offer. On his way home, Hine had second thoughts and, 40 miles away, pulled a U-turn and, returning to Paulson's farm, bought the horse, chip or no chip. The horse turned out to be blue-chip Skip Away, who ultimately won more than $9 mil and was valued at $15 mil at stud.

Another time, that right price was five dollars. That's the amount paid by Don Honig, a small-time St. Louis horse trader who, back in the nineteenth century, put down that amount in Grover Cleveland dollars on the nose and the rest of a horse. Adhering to Saint Jerome's advice never to look a "gift horse in the mouth," Honig took the animal back to his barn, all the while thinking such gifts of charity normally come encumbered with strings attached and bills to pay, otherwise, why had the owner parted with him for such a small amount? Giving his ebony stallion the name All Black, Honig waited for him to just lie down in his stall and die. Instead of dying, though, All Black showed plenty of life, eating up his bedding, kicking up his heels, and acting like anything but a sick horse. Prompted by his son, Honig finally took his horse out to the Fair Grounds where, at 100-to-1, he won his first race, then followed with another triumph at 500-to-1. The very next day, with a fresh bankroll of $50,000, Honig set up his own stable, courtesy of All Black, who would go on to win nineteen races in a row and provide Honig with the wherewithal to build his own racetrack at Gloucester, New Jersey, thus earning him the title "King of Gloucester." All for a five spot.

W hile small change can say a word or two every now and then, those at horse auctions had better be ready to make their checkbooks roar in loud clarion tones, as if they were megaphones.

For it is at those auctions conducted by the likes of Equine Spectrum, Barrett's, Heritage Place, Keeneland, Ocala Breeders, Pegasus Horse Auction, Tattersalls, and Fasig-Tipton that horses go for more than $1,200 per pound, putting them far ahead of caviar on the international market.

The auctions can be for weanlings, yearlings, two-year-olds, two-year-olds in training, or broodmares. But whatever they're for, they're for *real* money, bid by those whose wallets would be considered carry-on luggage.

Auctions are not only for the monied; the not-so-monied can apply, too. Several years ago, when Bill Schaftlein decided he wanted to own a race horse, he asked retired trainer Chester Hall, "How can I do it?" Hall responded, "The best way for a little fellow to get started is to go to the Keeneland yearling sales and buy a filly."

And so it is that at the coming-out party for platinum yearlings, the Keeneland Auction, can be found both the monied and non-monied walking around, sometimes accompanied by bloodstock agents, trainers, and vets, all with the ardor of astronomers in the hopes of discovering a new star in the chorus of heavens—as the Taylors did in 1975, buying Seattle Slew for $17,500 at a yearling sale or, on a more modest level, a $700 yearling of what Mary Simon described as "of peasant lineage": Alsab. The catalogues they carry describes each horse lot, with black type on the page reserved for such important items as to whether the horse's sire or dam, or grandsire, etc., had ever won a graded stakes race at an important track, important hints as to the horse's lineage. However, since the catalogues are printed well in advance of the sale, additional information is forthcoming from the signs posted on the horse's stall with a more up-to-date description of the horse—something along the lines of "Half brother won at Hollywood Park," or somesuch.

Because owners cannot just call up Fasig-Tipton for a stall, they turn to consignors who act as their sales agents. And, the bigger and best consignors not only have the most stalls, they have those closest to the main selling area, normally with the best horses, all the better for prospective buyers to see their wares— the lesser consignors being relegated to the proverbial back of the bus, somewhere, as one owner calls it, "in the boondocks."

The wheels of the racing gods grind slowly; and so it is that approximately three months before the auction the owners nominate their horse(s) by submitting a $500 entry fee as good faith that they will enter them in the sale. The owners are then visited by committee to inspect those nominated, grading them according to their conformation, stature, athleticism, physicality, and the like, while a second team visits to look at their pedigree.

Now, the consignor takes possession of the horses consigned to him, each working in his own way, his wonders to behold. Some take them sixty days in advance, working them out on treadmills and keeping them out of the sun. Others run them around, running them uphill for food and water, or vice versa, to keep them in good shape. And, in the olden days, before blood tests for steroids had yet to be perfected, a few even used steroids on yearlings to flesh them out—all in the name of making their horses look better so they could be shown to their best advantage.

Come the sale, the prospective buyers roam around the sales pavilions, asking the consignors to "bring them out, please," telling him which lot they wish to see ("Lot 1404 . . . Lot 1818," as indicated by the catalogue.) Only a small percentage of the buyers have gone down to look at the horses beforehand, maybe 1 to 2 percent will visit farms like Clairborne. Sometimes blood-stock agents for heavy hitters go in their stead.

As the horse is produced from the stall the buyer, with the eye of a recruiting sergeant, watches the horse as he/she walks, making tight turns and figure eights to make sure they don't paddle out or toe in. Some even check the footprints, seeing where the right front hoof lands, then the rear right, and how far the stride of the horse is, keeping the horse out for as long as they wish to look at it. Others look at the musculature, the posture, the conformation. One owner makes sure there is no excessive flex in the horse's legs or that the horse's legs aren't too straight, exerting stress on the tendons, and increasing the animal's tendency to break down. There are, of course, exceptions to every rule. Assault had a club foot deformity at birth, which didn't stop him from becoming one of *Forbes* magazine's all-time four-footed money earners. Or, John Henry, who had a conformation defect called "calf-kneed," or "back at the knees." And, according to trainer Lucien Laurin, the genes from his sire, Bold Ruler, shot right through to Secretariat, both having weaknesses in their right front foot.

But, as the saying goes, looks can be deceiving. Or, as trainer John E. Madden once said, "You can never tell how far a frog will jump by looking at him." So it is that had but many of racing's all-time greats been subjected to these so-called beauty inspections, their talents would have been discounted at far less than face value. Take the great Seabiscuit, who was such an unprepossessing horse that, if he had been inspected in such a manner, he wouldn't have brought the proverbial sou; or Hall of Famer Sysonby, who was a squat, homely animal, described by his groom as "a common, cheap-looking, lop-eared colt"; or Hall of Famer Roamer, whose looks begot this line from the trainer and writer Mose Goldblatt: "If he were led into a sales ring and none realized who he was, he would sell for $200." And then there was John Henry, who bloodied himself in his stall bouncing off the walls before the sale and came into the ring looking a mess; he sold for just $1,100.

Next, it's the veterinarian's turn. Horses have an enormous nerve in their head that extends all the way down and circles back and, if the right side becomes paralyzed inside the mouth or "flaps," the horse makes noises that sound like a trumpet, or, as the vets call it, "broken wind," impairing its breathing. To check for this defect, the vet inserts a three-and-one-half-foot scope down the horse's nose to examine the voice box and the flaps to see if the horse has a weak or flaccid epiglottis. Some more jaundiced buyers have their vets use a heart scope to test a horse's blood flow in its left ventricle to see if it is pumping the correct amount of oxygenated blood into its body. And then there was the Japanese owner Hiroshi Fujita, who had his vet check the horse's left fore-ankle, and when the bone scan and X rays came back showing a defect, rescinded his $1.4 mil purchase of a two-year-old who turned out to be the great Unbridled's Song.

After days of analyzing everything but a horse's SAT score, the prospective buyers and their agents and trainers are prepared and know which horse lot to bid on, and which wouldn't give them enough thought to cause a headache. And, if not, seek confirmation from others. (However, some, like trainer D. Wayne Lukas, won't look at the horses beforehand, preferring merely to stand at the gate to the circular paddock behind the auction ring and, as the horses walk past him, he watches and makes notes.)

Finally, the twelve-day sale is at hand, and most of those bidding take their seats on the chairs fronting the ring. Others, however, prefer to stand in the back, watching the auction on TV monitors and, looking as if they belonged in Madame Tussaud's waxworks, make subtle head and hand movements visible to auction agents without being seen by other bidders. It depends on where you stand, who sees you, and who has looked at you as to how you'll bid; most active bidding, which rachets up the price, is between two bidders, not three, four, or more. Even as some of the so-called heavy hitters try to merge into the scenery, unseen, the consignor of a horse that has been checked out by a particular bidder will pay a runner to sleuth on the bidder to see if he's bidding—and sometimes tweak the price upward.

The 3,500 or so lots are presented according to their presentation listing in the catalogue, and, depending upon the auction and the consignor, are identifiable by the numbers on their hips, or reins, or none at all, with the select horses going on sale during the first two days, followed, on days three through five, by those almost as good and, after that, in the words of one buyer, "it's catch as catch can."

With three paddocks in the back of the auction ring, the horses are brought into the ring. And, as they are, the horses, in sort of an equine traffic jam, are being brought from their stalls ten lots away into the paddocks in the rear. Then, asfastasyoucanreadthis, it's wham, bam, thank-you ma'am, the gavel comes down, and *Next!*

The purchaser, who has been subjected to his own scrutiny and credit check before the sale, signs a sales slip, and takes the horse quickly, the obligation for the horse not passing to the buyer until he takes the horse off the grounds.

However, there are exceptions. If the would-be purchaser doesn't pay within the allotted period of time, he receives a letter two to three weeks later with interest added to the amount; if he doesn't pay, period, the auction house shoulders the amount and pays the seller. Then there are "reserves," those amounts owners put on their horses to protect the horse from going too cheaply; if the bidding doesn't reach the required amount, the owner exercises his right of buy back. Peter Fuller did that at the 1967 Fasig-Tipton horses-in-training auction at Hialeah, buying back Dancer's Image for $26,000 when the horse's reserve price was an unmet $35,000—thus the notation "RNA" in the auctioneer's booklet, for "Reserve Not Attained."

One of the most famous purchases ever made at auction was the one made by Samuel Riddle in 1918. As Mary Simon wrote in *Racing Through the Century,*

> World War I was then at full boil, with more than a million American troops risking their lives on the battlefields of Europe. Under the circumstances, it seemed unthinkable to Major August Belmont II that he remain at home in the pastoral safety of his farm, Nursery Stud, planning matings and watching young thoroughbreds grow up. He chose instead to support his country in war and thus announced the sale of his entire yearling crop without reserve at the upcoming August Saratoga sales. Belmont's patriotic sacrifice cost him far more than he could possibly have anticipated, for among the twenty-one Nursery yearlings auctioned off was a colt like no other the American turf had ever seen—or would ever see.

The colt, already named by Mrs. Belmont to honor her husband, was Man o' War. And Riddle, a relative newcomer to the sport, became, in the words of Simon, "arguably the luckiest man who ever raised a finger to bid," purchasing the all-time great for $5,000, which prompted Riddle to say immediately after the sale, "This is the cheapest horse ever sold."

"Cheapest" has not always been an adjective used to describe purchases made at auctions; more oft than not, the figures tossed around are closer to 10-digit telephone numbers, with lots of zeros and commas thrown in. Just seven years after Riddle's $5,000 purchase, a Man o' War yearling filly begot $50,500, then an American auction record.

That was during the 1920s, a time when the economy was booming and newly minted money talked and talked loudly. Come the Depression and, suddenly, the Equinomics changed, and money, when it was heard, was reduced to a bare whisper. Yearling average sales plummeted by 75 percent.

It has always been thus, with horse sales tied to the economy: the healthier the economy, the healthier the prices bid for horses. After World War II, yearling average sales soared, then, by the mid-1950s, set all-time records and, by the 1970s, a dozen yearlings were sold for $1 mil or more. Skip to the early '80s and the average for yearlings peaked at more than $40,000, almost a fourfold increase over prices a decade earlier. With the market crash of 1987, came foreign money. By 1995, Japanese money accounted for almost half that spent at auctions.

The next big wave of foreign buyers were the Irish breeders, and those from the Dubai and Saudi Arabia, the Maktoums and Prince Ahmed bin Salman, respectively, both of whom cut an expensive swath through the yearling sales, paying princely sums to buy the best stock available and enjoying almost immediate success.

However, by the second year of the twenty-first century, with the death of the prince, the hyperventilating dot.com boom bursting with barely a whimper, and the economy going into the hamper, the yearling market similarly declined, especially the top echelon. Commenting on the depressed yearling market, trainer Nick Zito said, "What is it you read about in the papers every day? Criminals. Scandals. Which meant it wasn't real money to begin with." But it *is* real money that is evident at the auctions. And real money has a way of making itself heard.

As the vans pulled away, lumbered with their precious cargo purchased at the auction, the owners, too, are lumbered—with expectations and, more important, responsibilities.

Over and above the obvious responsibility of feeding and caring for their newly purchased stock, they also have to purchase insurance to cover them, from mortality insurance to major medical and surgical coverage and several other classifications running the gamut from owners' legal liability insurance to theft.

There is one more responsibility, a right and rite of ownership: the naming of their new acquisition.

It's not so much a question of "What's in a name?" as what's not. The Jockey Club oversees the naming of horses and their set of rules, some fourteen in all, make creativity difficult. Their list of admonitions limits the number of letters in a name, prohibiting the use of names of dead people unless approval has been granted, copyrights, commercial names, initials, numbers, and almost everything else, including suggestive, vulgar, or obscene names. Still, despite their list of thou-shalt-nots, every now and then some mischievous owner will slip a name past with a double entendre, like Hezaputz or Bodacious Tatas.

Some take the easy way out. Colonel E. R. Bradley, who had a fixation with the letter *B*, as in Bradley, named all his horses with names starting with the letter: Blue Lockspur, Brokers Tip, Burgoo King, Bimelech, Black Helen, Blade O' Time, Busher, Baby-League, Bubbling Over, and Behave Yourself.

Others are given an extension of their forebears, much as fathers name their sons junior or II; Unbridled's Song, sired by Unbridled; War Emblem, sired by Our Emblem; Bold Forbes, sired by Bold Ruler; Slew of Gold, sired by Seattle Slew; Dancer's Image, sired by Noor's Image; and Alysheba, sired by Alydar. Then there are those names that take both parents into consideration, such as Native Dancer, whose sire was Polynesian and whose dam, Geisha.

Sometimes the horse is named for someone. Mrs. Allaire duPont honored her friend, Mrs. Kelso Everett, by naming her horse Kelso after her; Admiral Gene Markey called his chestnut colt Alydar, a contraction of what Mrs. Markey once called Prince Aly Khan, "Aly, darling"; Admiral Markey, again, called his favorite filly Our Mims, after his daughter, Melinda; and 1929 Derby winner Clyde Van Dusen was named for his trainer, Clyde Van Dusen.

There are those names that are taken probably only because Spike Jones took the name "Beetlebaum" first, such as Giles Brophy naming a horse Furthest Point—after having the name Oh So Far turned down—because the horse was quartered three-quarters of a mile away in the barn space in the back at an auction, and he had to go the edges of the stalls to find him; or Alfred Vanderbilt, who bought a mare named Miyako and assumed Miyako was a Japanese name so, when she had a filly by Discovery, he called it Geisha; or Genuine Risk, a name submitted by Diana Firestone to mirror her uncertainty about the filly's chances.

Some of the most imaginative names came from, of all people, the man called "the establishmentarian's establishmentarian,"

Jockey Club
Criteria for Name Exclusion

1. Initials such as C.O.D., F.O.B., etc.;

2. Names ending in "filly," "colt," "stud," "mare," "stallion," or any similar horse-related term;

3. Names consisting entirely of numbers, except numbers above 30 may be used if they are spelled out.

4. Names ending with a numerical designation such as "2nd" or "3rd," whether or not such a designation is spelled out;

5. Names of persons unless written permission to use their name is on file with The Jockey Club;

6. Names of "famous" people no longer living unless approval is granted by the Board of Stewards of The Jockey Club;

7. Names of "notorious" people;

8. Names of race tracks or graded stakes races;

9. Recorded names such as assumed names or stable names;

10. Names clearly having commercial significance, such as trade names;

11. Copyrighted material, titles of books, plays, motion pictures, popular songs, etc., unless the applicant furnishes The Jockey Club with proof that the copyright has been abandoned or that such material has not been used within the last five years;

12. Names that are suggestive or have a vulgar or obscene meaning; names considered in poor taste; or names that may be offensive to religious, political or ethnic groups.

13. Names that are currently active either in the stud or on the turf, and names similar in spelling or pronunciation to such names, see 6(E); and

14. Permanent names and names similar in spelling or pronunciation to permanent names.

Source: Copyright © The Jockey Club. All rights reserved.

Ogden Phipps, chairman of the Jockey Club who, with tongue not removed far from cheek, named a daughter of War Admiral Busanda, shorthand for the U.S. Navy's Bureau of Supplies and Accounts. And went on to name her offspring Bupers, a contraction for the Bureau of Personnel. Phipps even went so far as to give the name Open Hearing to a colt by Court Martial, setting a new stand for cheeky irreverence when it came to naming horses.

Then there was Allen Brian, who needed a name for a three-year-old filly he co-owned, and named her Buffythecenterfold, the maximum number of letters allowed, in honor of Buffy Tyler, the *Playboy* Playmate of the Month in November 2000.

Proof that the name game can be played by anyone, in or out of racing, was best illustrated by a contest conducted by the *Washington Post's* Style section in which readers were asked to mate any two Kentucky Derby-eligible horses and come up with a name for their foal. Two of the winning entries were the mating of Yeti with White Bronco, their foal to be named Abominable Slowman, and The Toy Man with Hail to the Hero, their offspring to be known as F.A.O. Schwartzkopf.

But, whatever the name, the new owner hopes their purchase brings them fortune, if not fame, both at the track and, later, in the breeding shed.

As Secretariat bade farewell to his adoring New York fans and awaited shipment, FOB, to his new home at Claiborne Farm in Paris, Kentucky, where he would begin his new career at stud, sportswriter Si Burick, taking note of his change in lifestyle, couldn't resist writing, "He's everything I'm not. He's young; he's beautiful; he has lots of hair; he's fast; he's durable; he has a large

bank account; and his entire sex life is before him." And there, affixed to the door of his stall, was a *billet-doux* in the form of a postcard, reading, "I can't wait," signed Fiji, one of the broodmares in
his new harem.

The retirement to stud of Secretariat, a superhorse who set
records every time hoof hit track, was big news for an industry as
concerned with the breeding of horses as with the racing of them,
to the continuance of racing's life cycle by a horse of whom vet-
eran journalist Charles Hatton wrote, "I've never seen perfection
before. Secretariat's only point of reference is himself." For, if
Secretariat was the best of the best, then his progeny, or so the
reasoning went, would also be the best of the best. For that has always been the basic goal of breeders: not just the propagation of
the species, but the improvement of the breed.

Unlike most sciences and quasi-sciences, the exact date equine
genetics began is only somewhat traceable, most experts subscrib-
ing to a date somewhere back to right after the year Zip, the late
seventeenth and early eighteenth centuries when three desert
horses, called the Foundation Sires—the Byerley Turk, the Darley
Arabian, and the Godolphin Arabian—were brought into England
by various and sundry means, and employed to build the best breed
of equine athlete possible. The first stone to hit the American
breeding waters was the Epsom Derby winner Diomed, bought on
the cheap for $220 in Continental currency and brought over to
serve as America's version of the Foundation Sire. In ever-widening
circles, his efforts begot an entirely new breed of racehorse, one
with greater speed, taller and heavier bodies, and more stamina
than their British cousins.

And when, some fifty years later, Diomed's great-great-
grandson, appropriately named Lexington and born on a farm in
the bluegrass region of central Kentucky, came along to carry
Diomed's legacy and genetic links—reigning as America's leading sire sixteen times—Kentucky's place as home of the thoroughbred breeding industry was established.

According to *Thoroughbred Times*, by the end of the nineteenth century, Kentucky had become the heart of America's thoroughbred business. The number of foals registered by the Jockey Club totaled 3,784 and stud fees soared. However, by the end of the first decade of the twentieth century, anti-gambling legislation was on the march and sires worth thousands only a few years before couldn't be given away. And so it was that breeders began exporting their sires to England with more 1,500 going abroad, including more than 20 champions, some never to return. In retaliation, Britain's Jockey Club, overseeing racing in England, where it was not just a sport but an institution, passed the Jersey Act in 1913, barring American lines from their General Stud Book and, in effect, creating two separate lines—one for British horses and another for American thoroughbreds thought to be unworthy of the British Stud Book. By the next year, with England at war, the trend had reversed, and America became an aggressive importer of the best bloodstock money could buy.

When Man o' War, a horse with unassailable pedigree, was retired to stud on Samuel Riddle's Kentucky Farm in 1921, where he sired seven of his eight champions in his first four foal crops, and overall sixty-four stakes winners, setting progeny earnings records just as he had on the track, Kentucky's place in the breeding sun was one again reestablished.

Jersey Act or no—which would ultimately be repealed in 1949, having served only to put British breeding interests at a disadvantage—the American breeding industry went on its merry way, stork quotations for newborn foals rising to 5,137 by 1930, 6,316 by '39, and more than 10,000 by '57, its numbers in lockstep with the burgeoning purses of the races themselves. The growth had been fueled by the purchase of Bienheim II in 1936 by a syndicate organized by A. B. Hancock, Sr. and the retirement to stud of supersire Bull Lea—prompting trainer Ben Jones to say, "Breed 'em all to Bull Lea."

After a century-plus of selective breeding, the height of the average American thoroughbred had increased by eight inches. Moreover, because shorter races had taken the place of the previous century's four-mile marathons, thoroughbreds now were bred for speed; their average speed increased by some twelve seconds a mile.

The breeding boom reached a peak in the 1950s—the first of many—when Nashua became the first horse to be syndicated for the theretofore unheard price of $1 million. (A syndicate is an association of approximately forty people with each shareholder entitled to one "cover" or "season," a mating each year with one of their mares with the syndicated sire in return for their investment, sometimes the home farm and the trainer getting one as well.)

Then came a new wrinkle to the world of breeding: the introduction of a second season by Irish breeders. No longer was a sire confined to just one season in America—now they could do their begetting in dual hemispheres, as Irish and, then, Japanese breeders shipped them off to southern climes for a second season. An active sire could double his pleasure, and double his fun, servicing as many as 175 mares in two seasons, dramatically increasing his value.

Even while the breeding industry was awaiting his much-heralded arrival, Secretariat was setting standards on the track as well as in the world of syndication, having been syndicated for $6.08 mil, a sum equal to many Third World countries' GNP, with each share purchased for $190,000. He more than preserved his negotiability with his thirty-one-length blowout victory in the 1973 Belmont—proof that when history repeats itself, the price goes up.

The life Secretariat had to look forward to was one Nashua's groom had so eloquently described for his charge when he listed his duties: "Eatin', sleepin', runnin', and making love all your life. That's it! Nothing more, nothing less." And a life Hoist the Flag, when he was vanned straight from Belmont to that large breeding farm outside Paris, Kentucky, Claiborne Farms, had spelled out for him in letters writ large on the back page of the New York *Daily News*, TO PARIS FOR OO LA LA. All Secretariat had to do was fulfill those duties, to sow his wild oats, and more, in the name of providing horsedom with, if not more Secretariats, then at least those with Secretariat's championship genes.

Breeding is, at best, an imprecise science. Take the case of Colonel E. R. Bradley, who believed a story told him by an old Indian woman of her husband's dream on his deathbed that were Bradley to mate his main sire, Black Toney, with a common mare, he would have a Derby winner. Bradley did exactly that and the pairing produced Black Gold, winner of the 1924 Derby. And trainer John E. Madden, decrying the lack of breeding in Sarazen, the 1924–25 Horse of the Year, said: "When a man can breed a quarter horse to a plow mare and get a horse that can beat everything in America, it's time for me to sell out."

For those who haven't taken Animal Husbandry 101 (and for several of those who have, and have been thrown out of school for practicing it), the process of breeding is one of getting the mares to ovulate—sometimes even giving them drugs to induce—then, when they are in season or heat, mating them to a sire. However, since only about half the horses become pregnant, an ultrasound is used fourteen days afterward to see if the mare took.

Breeding is now facing as serious a problem as any it has ever had to cope with: that of mare reproductive loss syndrome (MRL), which has cut the gross foal crop nearly in half. The spate of foal deaths that first occurred in the spring of 2001 has been attributed to everything from cyanogetic compounds to fungal organisms, to caterpillars from surrounding trees; but none of these have yet been proven to be the cause, and MRL now threatens the tradition-bound Keeneland July auction.

Inasmuch as the gestation period for a horse is approximately 340 days, owners don't want horses born in the last two-thirds of the year because of the universal birthdate for all thorough-breds—January 1, regardless of the actual birthdate, which means you'll never forget a horse's birthday. If a horse is born in, say, the autumn, it will be one year old in just a few months and will be racing against other two-year-olds a year later, giving away more than a small chunk of age—something like a sixth grader racing against far more developed twelfth graders.

Years ago, Red Smith told the story of a horse named Mary V., not an official member of the Triple Crown winner Whirlaway's court, who was sneaked into Whirlaway's bed-barn by someone or other far ahead of the normal breeding season. The colt, a leggy son, was born late in the year and Warren Wright, master of Calumet Farms, was more than upset, fearing that such a puny horse would make his champion stallion look bad, even threatening not to register the foal. However, Charles Fisher, owner of Dixiana Farm, bought what Smith called "Whirlaway's love child" and named it First Whirl, after its old man. Because of his age handicap, it was believed the youngster would not run until he was officially three years of age, but he was entered in a race at Keeneland and won going away. It was to be his only win.

Over the years, several breeding theories have evolved and the vet process has gotten better. Still, breeding is a sometime thing, prompting the moral reflection that life is made up of equal parts smiles, satisfactions, and sniffles. Smiles and satisfactions when the names Man o' War, Bull Lea, Alydar, Bold Ruler, Seattle Slew, Sir Galahad II, Count Fleet, and others are mentioned, all of whom have champions in their gets. However, sniffles predominate when the names of great champions like Tom Fool (known as "the Celebrated Celibate"), Assault, Omaha, and, more recently, Cigar, have been mentioned—all of whom came up empty.

The number of great champions who have produced champions of their own can be written on the small message portion of a postcard, with more than enough room left over for an oversized postage stamp and a picture of the breeding farm itself. Although it seems sacrilegious to consider the alternative, contrary to expectations, Secretariat hardly set the same standard in the breeding barn that he set on the racetrack. For when Diana Firestone paired her remarkable filly Genuine Risk with Secretariat to produce what she hoped would be an *überhorse*, the pairing failed twice: the first time, the result was a stillborn colt; the second time, it didn't take.

Call it *kismet* or being born under a particular star or anything you like, up to and including "the Curse of the Bambino," but the bread some breeders cast upon the waters comes back bread pudding with fine cream sauce, while, for others, it's mere crumbs. And, thus far, outside of his grandson, Chief's Crown, and his great-grandson, Charismatic, Secretariat has done little to warrant his being included in that great pantheon of sires, along with Man o' War, Bull Lea, and the rest. (Even when a son of Secretariat was sold for $1.5 mil, trainer John Nehrud, commenting on the price of the great sire's yearling, said "A horse is worth $50 and what the traffic will bear.")

It has been estimated that, from the time a foal draws its very first breath, the odds are a thousand to one it will find its way to the starting gate of the Derby. Others say the odds are much higher, since the number of thoroughbreds foaled in 2000 was 37,587. Either way, the odds of getting to the Derby and having a Secretariat, or even one of his offspring, is higher. Much higher. Still, those up in Millionaires' Row would be more than happy to have paid the $600 nominating fee and the $30,000 fee just to get one into the starting gate.

The party up in the Millionaires' Row had wound down; many of those who had joined it after it had started had left before it was finished. The rest, having finished telling their Rubaiyats of the Juleps had laid down their cups before they were in them, all the better to watch what was happening on the track below. For the bugler had sounded his call and Stephen Foster's anthem had been played and, now, racing's fashion show, the post parade, was taking place, with the horses, several of whom had gathered their rosebuds whilst they might in the preps on their way to the Run for the Roses, as excited as those in the stands, frisking their way around the track.

Any minute now the Most Exciting Two Minutes in Sports would begin. (Or, as one attendee put it a few years ago, "The tension is boring.")

And then, there they were in the starting gate and, nanoseconds later, the gate had sprung and they were off. And everywhere people were jumping up and down, like rice dancing in a saucepan, as the horses came romping around the track. As they came into the stretch, some so close to the promised land they could almost touch it, while those in the rear as close to the finish line as Pittsburgh native Stephen Foster was to Louisville when he wrote "My Old Kentucky Home," the owners of the frontrunners erupted in a spontaneous combustion of hosannahs, sounding like one of the explosions that kill five or six bystanders, urging on their horses.

Then, suddenly, it was over. And the winning owners were greeted with more backslapping than could be found at a Shriners' convention as they picked up their congratulations. Now, only one more thing need be done: They had to go down to the winner's circle for the traditional postprandial goings-on to pick up the winner's gold Derby Trophy.

Going back to 1511, trophies for the winner have been a racing tradition; the first was a silver bell given to the winner at Chester, England. In 1609, it was decided to convert the bell into three silver cups; in 1623, the three cups were combined into "one faire silver cuppe of the value of £8," according to records of the day.

Throughout racing history, the hardware given the winning owner has been as important to them as the Congressional Medal of Honor and the Nobel Prize medal to their winners. For it means more by far than its intrinsic value; it symbolizes their having climbed to the top of the racing mountain. For that one shining moment—and, in memory, forever.

As the comedian Joe E. Lewis once said, "Horse racing is the only sport that gives out more gifts than you can get at a housewarming or a wedding." To prove Joe E. right, racing gives out more than the union minimum, with such precious and semiprecious trophies and cups given out to victors as the Queen's Plate, given to the winner of the great eponymous Canadian race, the Keeneland Julep Cups or Beakers, the Breeders' Futurity Tray, the Preakness Woodlawn Vase, and the Breeders' Cup Trophy—the last of which is not a cup, plate, or goblet, but a replica of the Torrie horse created in Florence by Giovanni da Bologna, in the late 1580s.

Many of those same trophies were won by racing's most dominant stable, Calumet Farms. When Calumet declared bankruptcy in the 1980s, more than 550 of those valuable trophies became part of the estate to be auctioned off for the benefit of the creditors. While they were momentarily displayed at the Kentucky Horse Park in Lexington, the court-appointed auction house, Sotheby's, prepared for the auction and appraised the Calumet Farms Collection at $1 million, a figure local corporations raised to protect one of racing's most valuable legacies, Calumet's trophies. However, when one of the creditors' attorneys saw other trophies for no-name horses being sold for as much as $1,500 apiece, he petitioned the bankruptcy judge as to why solid gold cups for horses like Whirlaway and Citation were appraised by Sotheby's at a mere $20 apiece. The court thereupon replaced Sotheby's with Guernsey's and, after reappraising the collection as being worth $3 mil, the president of Guernsey's, Arlan Ettinger, worked with the local corporations to save the collection for Kentucky and the Kentucky Horse Park, preserving Kentucky's rich history.

But the worth of a trophy or cup or whathaveyou is not measured in dollars. Take the time Jack Amiel, owner of Count Turf, winner of the 1951 Derby, carried the Derby Trophy like a bowl of goldfish on his lap on a train all the way back from Louisville to New York, telling one and all who got too close, "Look out! You'll scratch it."

This is what every owner that first Saturday in May wants—a chance to say, "Look out! You'll scratch it!" as they carry the Derby Trophy away.

D. Wayne Lukas preps his 1996 Derby entrant Prince of Thieves at Churchill Downs *(Copyright © Getty Images, Getty Images North America).*

3

THE TRAINERS

Owners may come and go, some having picked Patrick Henry's second choice, while others who were just in the sport for the parties and social life have picked up their marbles and gone home. But trainers remain. For they are the factotums who make the sport work, the most indispensable part of the equation.

They are there every year in the Derby winner's circle, accepting plaudits and having their pictures taken, legendary names printed on the right-hand side of the program, like D. Wayne Lukas, Neil Drysdale, Nick Zito, Jack Van Berg, Mack Miller, Bob Baffert, Lynn Whiting, Carl Nafzger, and John Ward, among others. Celebrities all, in a world where the word *celebrity* used to mean anyone who had been seen on television at least twice, and now has come to mean one of the trainers of a leg of the Triple Crown.

These are the trainers who have the ears of the biggest owners, who garner frequent-flyer miles traveling between their stables— sometimes as many as three, in the belief, as Oscar Wilde said, that "Three addresses inspire confidence, even in a tradesman"—and who are, at least to the outside world, the epitome of a trainer.

Throughout the long and winding road of racing there have been may famous trainers—names, many lost to living memory, like James Rowe Sr., John Hyland, H. Guy Bedwell, Sunny Jim Fitzsimmons, John E. Madden, Max Hirsch, Samuel Hildreth, Ben Jones, Jimmy Jones, Hirsch Jacobs, R. H. "Red" McDaniel, Charlie Whittingham, Woody Stephens, Mesach Tenney, John Nerud, Laz Barrera, LeRoy Jolley, and John Veitch. But for every one of these, there are thousands more who have toiled in relative anonymity, their love for the sport and for their horses equal to that of any of the big-name trainers.

Far from the klieg lights and media attention showered on such celebrity trainers, many of whom continue to rewrite the legend each and every Derby, is an entire world of unknown trainers, thousands more, from large to one-horse stables, winning races in relative obscurity and soldiering on merely in an attempt to make ends meet, hoping against hope that one day one of their horses will enable them to join the ranks of celebrity trainers. Every now and then, something like that happens, as when Cam Gambolati's horse Spend a Buck won the 1985 Derby. But since there were about 73,000 starters, all told, in the United States and Canada in 2002, and only 25 percent or so of them ever see the inside of the winner's circle, the Gambolatis are few and far between.

The lot of a trainer is not an easy one, the very word *trainer*, an olde English term, being a misnomer covering a complex job description. He is, in turn, one part teacher, one part healer, one part planner, one part weatherman, one part counselor, one part horse trader, one part manager, and one part general handyman. Johnny Longdon, who both rode and trained Derby winners, once said that being a trainer involved "a lot of pressure and a lot of headaches." And they weren't even in the job specs.

There are more sides to being a trainer than those on Rubik's Cube. Be he a trainer who runs a large stable or a small one, he is the man responsible for the care and feeding of his horses; acting as a major domo overseeing his own staff, from muckrakers and stable swipes to grooms to riders and exercise boys to assistant trainers and even vets; interacting with the owners of the horses in his stable; adding to his own stable; and, in some cases, acting as a bird-dog or scout for owners in their acquisition of new stock. All in all, a trainer's job is one of wearing many hats and keeping twenty-eight balls in the air at once, two of which are his own.

At the core of his duties is the horse. For the horse is not only his primary concern—it is his ticket. The trainer will feed his horses, nurse them, stand by them in sickness and in health, work them out, and train them—sometimes pleading and cajoling with them and, in more cases than he'll ever admit, spoiling them worse than his favorite child, buying them the best shoes, vets, and feed money can buy and even bribing or rewarding them with candy bars or other sweets—Kelso loving chocolate sundaes.

Trainers can be either heavy-handed or velvet gloved, Captain Bligh or Rebecca of Sunnybrook Farm when it comes to training a horse. Sunny Jim Fitzsimmons never coddled one in his care, saying only, "You've got to get them to do what they're raised for. Spoil 'em, and you're ruining your chances." To prove his point, he would take one of his star pupils, Gallant Fox, and put him in workouts that ranged from long gallops to a series of brutal speed dashes. Others treat a horse as one of their own, almost a son, babying them along. The proof, to not coin a phrase, is in the pudding. The payoff is the winner's circle, and whatever it takes to get them there is the right way.

However, it costs as much to feed a Kelso as it does a cheap claiming horse. And many's the trainer who, after charging the owners to stable a horse and pay for the vet bills and shoes, doesn't make enough bread to spread on his role. This trainer's constantly on a financial tightrope trying to make a living from the dribs and drabs offered in low-level races at lesser tracks— that is, if his horse wins. One trainer, suggesting that one part of the problem lay with the owners, said: "Boy, they are fast to the winner's circle and even faster to the pay window, but real slow in paying their bills."

There is no need to embroider; the truth makes all things plain. There are a goodly number of trainers who know adversity, but who also know that it is but an invisible pane of glass separating victory from defeat and, with no unconditional surrender to undeniable facts, continue on in the hope that where they once prospected they will now hit paydirt. For one of the most recurrent themes in dramaturgy is the overcoming of such adversity, even though silent heresies of reason should tell them that their hopes of filling to an inside straight are small, indeed. Still, such indulgences are normally accorded in the natural order of human nature. For that is the world of the trainer, a world of hope and of pursuing their dreams despite omens and obstacles, knowing that the great equalizer is their horse crossing the finish line first.

While some of the racing world arise at the crack of ice, the trainer is up at the unsociable hour of five and, in a semi-coma of sleep, on his way to the track where, after enough high-octane coffee to enable him to walk on Lake Erie, he settles down to his morning's work. The first order of business is checking with the other members of the dawn patrol or his staff about the health of the horses and their feed—Allen Jerkins even taking great care to taste the horses' feed before giving it to them.

Painting a word picture as well as a tattered dictionary will allow each and every barn along shed row is different. Each is diverse and, depending on the makeup of the stablehands, the music that soothes the nonsavage beasts, both horse and human, may take the form of salsa, mariachi, rock, rap, golden oldies, or any other form of liquid architecture that adds to the aura of the barn area. There are invariably the pets, a managerie which may consist of ponies, ducks, geese, dogs, cats, chickens, or whatever animal life is needed to provide company and comfort to the horses. Sometimes, the pets can be disruptive, as when Angel Cordero went to visit his mount and had to fight off a chicken who was roosting on his horse's back and refused to get off 'til both he and the horse were fed. And there is the redolent aroma of horses, hay, saddle soap, and liniment everywhere.

There are so many people working in and around shed row that one is tempted to cop a line from *Butch Cassidy and the Sundance Kid*, asking, "Who are those people?" For the trainer's fiefdom, depending upon the size of his stable, is a small village, including an assistant trainer, exercise riders, grooms, stall muckers, hot walkers, valets to horses, braiders for rainy days, and on and on, both veterans and "greenies," all performing tasks necessary to getting the horses ready for their two-plus moments in the sun—or rain.

Recently, more and more women have entered into the ranks of trainers or their support staff, a growing trend which may be traceable to the 1970s, an era when women entered the realm of the sport, or maybe an affection for the horses themselves, attributed in part to the residual feeling for the fallen filly great, Ruffian. With a majority of those at equine vet schools now females and a growing number visible on shed row, it's a long step from the time when Mary Hirsch, the eminently qualified daughter of famed trainer Max Hirsch, was first denied a trainer's license by the New York Jockey Club and then, two years later, in 1935, granted one in Illinois, becoming racing's first licensed female trainer. But make no mistake about it, these women are not there just because, in stable jargon, they're "lookers" but because, as one owner, after observing them working with horses, said, "Women are better with horses . . . more caring and gentler . . ." and in the words of one fellow backstretcher, "have far more patience."

For many, the beginning of their journey into the ranks of trainerdom starts here, most of the trainers come up through these ranks, gain on-the-job experience—the name everyone gives their mistakes—by serving in various capacities: As grooms (Frank Martin and LeRoy Jolley), jockeys (Johnny Longdon), hot walkers (Bobby Frankel), other types of racing (D. Wayne Lukas and Bob Baffert, quarter horse; James Maloney, steeplechase); or apprenticing for their fathers (Jimmy Jones).

Then there are the horses—not only horses of a different color, but different levels of skill as well. While some barns suffer an embarrassment of riches, others are less apt to house a stakes horse than a barnful of claimers, more Yellow Pages than Blue Book. However, as trainer John Nerud, who more than once had a horse of ignoble breeding by nothing out of nothing beat one with a preference for pedigree, said: "Don't tell me who he's by, just who he's passed by."

A stable's horses can run the gamut from some consistent check-getters, to some also-rans who also ran and are suffering from a prolonged absence from the winner's circle to a few pieces de resistance with diminished capacities, a couple who could be discharged for having viewed racing as a wasteful vocation, and those cobbled together with baling wire. It is this last group, those Emma Lazarus would have embraced, that trainers spend their mornings tending to, those sorely compromised by injury or suffering from a fever or some other malady making them as weak as day-old ginger ale.

Injuries are every trainer's constant companion, the horse being, in the words of one of racing's breeding patriarchs, Seth Hancock, "a poorly constructed animal." With reed-thin legs carrying 1,200 pounds and having less meat on them than can be found under a butcher's thumb, the horse's legs are susceptible to an entire list of equine ailments—enough to necessitate a book, Dr. O. R. Adams's *Lameness in Horses*.

Injuries may be the result of horses merely outrunning their bodies, their legs forfeiting the duties they had sworn to uphold, cracking or breaking under the strain—as when Great Ruler shattered a leg pulling up from a gallop; or when Ruffian, who, in her match race with Foolish Pleasure, snapped her leg, dying as she had run, on the lead. Or their fragility could be attributed to their genetic underpinnings, some pedigreed ancestors having peed in the gene pool—as seemed to be the case for Buckmaster's cracked foreleg, his mare, Busanda, having had three other foals who had broken their legs. Or to the surface of a track. Or to the trainer breaking down his horses by running them with problems.

Whatever the reason for their fragility, the horse is a frail piece of merchandise, suffering from a catalogue of ills and woes known only to horsekind. The list is neverending. You name it—if you can pronounce it, they've got it, ailments running the gamut from inflammations, infections, abscesses, hoof and coronary band problems, internal bleeding, bloatedness, et cetera, et cetera, et cetera, to just plain ol' shoe problems.

And, for a time, the barn takes on the look of an equine intensive-care ward as trainer and staff administer all manner of treatment to the stricken animal, ranging from merely tubbing the horse to giving it injections or poultices or ultrasound to administering a cabinet of drugs, including among others, Dimethyl suffoxide (DMSO) and phenylbutazone or "bute," the use of which, too close to the 1968 Derby, resulted in the disqualification of

Dancer's Image. The restriction, once in force in Kentucky, on using bute too close to race day, has since been changed. In fact, medication rules seem to change almost as often as phases of the moon, and stewards are forever updating trainers on new rules. Once, when stewards came to Mesh Tenney's stable to advise him of the new medication rules then in vogue that season, Tenney, in a don't-bother-me manner, brushed them off with: "Do you have any rules on hay and grain? Because if you don't, don't bother me. I'm not using any drugs. . . . I'm not going to, and I never have."

Allen Jerkins's Lourdes-like abilities of being able to turn cripples into winning horses is near legendary. On a lesser level, trainer Mitch Friedman claimed an unnoteworthy four-year-old named Brutally Frank, who came with no pretense nor pedigree but with a history of bad feet, and turned him into a winner by using glue-on shoes on the advice of his smithy, Ian McKinley, the alchemy taking, earning McKinley the nickname "the Foot Doctor."

Sometimes, the horse will merely tell the trainer when he is ready to run, his demeanor conveying his willingness. There are also horses who possess that indefinable quality called a will to run or heart, like "the Magnificent Invalid," John Henry, whose heroic efforts prompted his trainer, Ron McAnally, to say, "Do you suppose we could give some of my horses a piece of his heart while he's not using it to race?"

Whether whole or whole of heart, the secret is playing the horses as if they were cymbals; there is no need to know how to play them, just *when*. And to determine that *when*, the trainer must, in the words of one, "Just pay attention to the horse." Or, as trainer Red McDaniel said: "When a horse is ready to run, I run him often. There's no use leaving his race on the training track."

However, as many times as not, even a miracle fails to bring about the desired effect and, with the horse's legs up for adoption and natural prejudice running to four good legs and the horse having less than the required minimum, the horse has to be scratched.

Over and above treating the lame, the halt, and the blighted, a trainer must also attend to the various needs of his other horses, some of them dilettantes needing special attention. With some, little flirtations and compliments work; with others, the other end of the carrot—the stick—works best. The eccentricities and idiosyncrasies of horses can be triggered by new surroundings, the darkness, oddly colored stables, or companion ponies—or one thousand and one other things that set them off, making them highstrung and irritable.

While some horses are like Buckpasser—whom trainer Eddie Neloy once described as "a star that never missed a curfew, never had a contract dispute, and always showed up for training"— others are hard-core headcases, four-alarm problems who could qualify for a group discount from the American Psychiatric Association. These are the mean ones, those who bite, eat blankets, and knock down everything in the barn—sometimes even the barn itself. Forego, who became more belligerent than a gladiatorial hornet, would calm down when his owner, Martha Farish Gerry, showed up in the paddock area. However, sometimes, even more extreme measures than a spoonful of sugar may have to be taken to tame these terrors, the most extreme being gelding, or castration.

They reinvented the Exterminator wheel by gelding the horse. Postop, he not only became the dominant handicap horse of the decade, but also one of the most docile. Sportswriter John Hervey described Exterminator as possessing what he called a "calm" mood when he traveled and that "when the door of the boxcar was opened and he was summoned forth, he would step out and stand quietly, without even a halter being necessary."

No matter what sleight-of-hand or ministrations a trainer employs, his success ultimately lies in the hands of Lady Luck. How else to explain those trainers who always seem able to turn manure into money, while others have about as much of a chance of success as a down-on-his-luck pyromaniac sneezing on his last match?

Take the legendary trainer Sunny Jim Fitzsimmons, who had been an average, hardworking trainer for years and in one year became the trainer for both Belair Stud Farm and the Wheatley Stable. How that piece of good fortune happened was chronicled in Jimmy Breslin's book *Sunny Jim: The Life of America's Most Beloved Horseman*. According to Breslin, "On a Saturday afternoon in November of 1923, Mr. Fitz was coming into the paddock at Pimlico Race Track just as a man named William Woodward was leaving. Woodward was a quiet, austere man who had a mustache, straight, matted-down hair and a checkbook in his inside coat pocket that no fountain pen could ever whack out."

Woodward came up to Fitzimmons and, calling on his fine command of the English language, said only: "Fitz, I'd like to speak to you. Would you like to train my horses?" Fitzsimmons answered in equally succinct words, "Love it," and thus began a relationship, with portfolio and without contract, with the Belair Stud Farm that would last many a year and produce champions like Gallant Fox and Omaha, both Triple Crown winners. Or, take the time Willis Sharpe Kilmer owned a horse named Sun Beau whom he had entered in the 1918 Derby. But when Sun Beau broke down, Kilmer reluctantly took the advice of his trainer, Henry McDaniel, and entered another horse, Exterminator, who won in a romp. Or trainer Billy Turner, who had been waiting a lifetime for his coach and six to arrive, then "One day you just look up, and there he is"— the "he" being Seattle Slew.

It is almost as though that moth-eaten adage, "Hope can set you free. So can a damn fast, undefeated racehorse" applied only to certain trainers. Unfortunately, Lady Luck does not bestow her smile on all trainers. There are many for whom she has been no lady at all, those unlucky ones who, if their ship were about to come in, could be found at the train station.

For some, the only way to survive may be to cast their luck at the pari-mutuel windows. Writer Bill Barich tells of running into a trainer of his acquaintance at a Left Coast clubhouse bar. The trainer, who had walked around the rim of success but never tasted it, was now tasting the equivalent of embalming fluid and, by now, feeling its effect as well as the ravages of fate. Saddened of face and reddened of eye, his anguish straight out of the Book of Job, the trainer turned to Barich and tried to address him, but the words flowed like cement. Finally, when he did speak, in the words of Barich, "his boozy voice soughed like the wind" as he told his tale of woe. "I gave that horse everything he could want," the trainer belched, "and look what the bastard did to me." And with that, his fist unclenched and several hundred dollars of worthless tickets fluttered to the bar floor.

Nevertheless, those trainers who have gone through good times and those who have gone through perilous times, hitting every bump along the bottom, are members of the same fraternity, a fellowship with racing running deep in their blood. And so it was that, back in 1948, as a member of that fraternity, trainer W. Hal Bishop, at the time one of the leading trainers at Arlington Park, came across a fraternal member who was bereft as Robinson Crusoe without a boat. The trainer, knowing the deficiencies of the day would not be supplied by the morning, was down and out and unable to meet his payroll. On the spot, without a second's hesitation or interest asked, Bishop wrote the down-on-his-luck trainer a check for $5,000.

The trainer's world is one where, as they say, it's chicken today, feathers tomorrow for some. On the other hand is the hope-giving counterbalancing quote that keeps them all in the game: "Nobody with an untried two-year-old ever committed suicide." It's that kind of world.

Most trainers are 56/100ths percent purer than Ivory Soap and, regardless of whether their horses are running as if chained to Morpheus's slow carriage and wins unforthcoming, would rather pluck out an offending eye than resort to anything that would smack of rascality. Still, there have been those who have stepped on the banana peel of temptation, those very few who, grasping at any straw to stay the inevitable, have resorted to less than honorable ways of winning and cashing in bets.

The practice was prevalent back in the heyday of betting rings, when the country was race- and bet-mad and villainy was everywhere. Even amongst trainers. It was a day and age when, as A. J. Liebling described it, "horses went to the post frothing and preening like unto De Quincy's opium addict," when toxicologists were in full bloom and hophorses ran under stimulative medication. (It was even suggested that 1919 Triple Crown winner Sir Barton was, in the words of Red Smith, "coked to the eyes whenever he ran," his bright-eyed glaze making him look like a tilted pinball machine.)

For the first third of the twentieth century, larceny was everywhere, with such time-dishonored methods employed by unscrupulous trainers as masking a horse's condition, substituting speed ringers for notorious nondescripts, electrifying the beasts, clocking horses at less than their normal times, and administering drugs for which no testing process had yet been devised.

Those trainers who were known among their colleagues as "chemists" had an entire cabinetful of drugs to choose from, from heroin to caffeine to benzedrine, to just about anything else than can be concocted in a laboratory. The practice of "spitting on a horse's tongue" or administering "foo-foo powder" was as much psychological as performance enhancing, as evidenced by a story told by Jim Coleman, retailed to him by another trainer, Happy Anderson, about a colleague. Seems, according to Coleman, that a trainer sent his wife over to a neighboring "chemist's" barn to borrow a cup of sugar, in the form of heroin, for one of his horses. However, on the way back, the wife tripped and spilled the contents of the cup. Unperturbed, she merely opened up her compact and sprinkled some of her white face powder into the cup and delivered it, with nary a mention of the substitution. Well, the trainer gave the contents of the cup to the horse and the horse ran and won. "That's great stuff," the exuberant trainer said to his wife. "We'll have to borrow more the next time we want to win a bet."

There were other methods of pulling off a betting coup, one of which was knocking the favorite off the board by drugging him, or by inserting small pieces of sponge into his nasal cavities to restrict his air flow and make running more difficult. Or the more creative method of horse painting, altering a ringer's appearance, then substituting the camouflaged ringer for an inferior one, the preferred method being the use of henna dyes, which withstood rain, washing, and liniment applications.

But "touching up" was not frowned upon by members of the old guard who, in the words of Red Smith, "never accepted the notion that it was wrong to help a horse out." Nor a trainer so down on his luck that if he were dominoes, he would be a double-zero. To those with a charitable bent (or view), the trainer was regarded less as a blackguard than a survivor, it being believed in days of old that such trainers were not criminally motivated, but instead resorted to less-than-honest expediencies merely to pay their bills and care for their horses.

And, while many safeguards are now in place, including the tattooing of horses' lips and issuance of foal birth certificates, as well as an elaborate system of drug checking, some of these practices still exist, particularly down at the fairground level. Still, it is more a part of racing's past than present, those few trainers who indulged in such practices part of racing's Runyonesque history.

After finishing his many duties in the barn, the trainer normally repairs to his office, if he has one; otherwise, any spare space, up to and including a knee or muck pack will do nicely, thank you. There, one of the first things he does is consult the *Condition Book*, his bible for the "wheres" and "whens" of upcoming races, along with their requirements and purses. Careful reading enables the trainer to set up a schedule for his horses, pointing to particular races for particular horses. For instance, he may want to drop a sound horse down into a claiming race in an attempt to steal it, or decide which horses to ship out before their plates are cooled, or which distance race to dump one of his horses into, or which horse is the best candidate for a particular race, or merely follow the money breadcrumbs, moving his horses around to where he can make the most money.

After taking into consideration every determining factor of whether to enter a horse in a given race—some trainers, like Lyle Whiting, have earned a reputation for never entering a horse in a race unless they believe they had a good chance of winning—other factors, most notably, the competition, may come into play. Take the time famed trainer Max Hirsch, after tentatively agreeing to enter his great '40s horse Assault in a three-horse race against Armed and Stymie, decided against it. Hirsch's reasoning, which sounded like the end of an old limerick, about who "had the right to do what and which and to whom," went: I'll run against either of those horses, but not both together. A come-from-behind horse will beat a sprinter every time. But why stick Assault in there to beat himself whipping a fast horse like Armed only to get nailed from behind by a plodder like Stymie? So goes the wisdom of trainers. (Postscript: Assault would later race against Armed in a two-horse, $100,000 match race in September of '47 and be beaten by eight lengths.)

One of those old racetrack adages that dates back to the dawn of time, and probably before, goes: "There are horses for courses." And each trainer must know which courses best suit his horses. It's not exactly teaching a crab to walk straight; but still, with a horse's active usefulness or shelf life so short, a trainer must know what works best for his horses and point them in that direction. For instance, most sprinters, after a mile, put up the FOR HIRE sign and can be found leaning against the mile pole trying to catch their breath; thus, it would be folly to put them in distance races.

Just as there are horses for courses, so, too, are there trainers for horses, certain trainers with certain abilities for training horses for specific courses. For example, trainers with quarterhorse backgrounds, like Bob Baffert, excel in sprinters, as does Linda Rice with two-year-old horses. Sunny Jim Fitzsimmons won fifty-two races at more than ten furlongs, more than any trainer in history, and became known as a distance trainer. And Claude "Shug" McGaughey, who trains the Phipps horses, is known for his late-closing horses. And then there is Allen Jerkins, known as "the Giant Killer," who not only points his horses toward a given race, but manages to pull off upsets in those races, having beaten five-time Horse of the Year Kelso three times and Secretariat twice.

After mind wrestling with the *Condition Book*, the trainer's next order of early-morning business is business. Absent a secretary who can take down anything that comes up, as only the larger and more affluent trainers can afford, the trainer usually fills out the entry forms for the races he has chosen for his horses, types out the entries, prepares budgets for his owners, pays the ever-mounting bills for the stable, and posts them. One California trainer, swamped by the paperwork he had to process, was called up on charges by a state agency which cited him for paying his stable help in cash and not deducting the appropriate withholding taxes, and for improperly entering overtime pay. The trainer, pleading his case, was nonplused, answering, "Why not? I pay my accountant in cash."

Then, after checking the weather reports more times than Willard Scott, as well as the past performance charts of other horses in his horses' races and the condition of the track, it's off to breakfast—whether in his own stable or in a communal mess hall with other trainers, where the main course is shop talk.

The morning half over, it's back to the stable-hyphen-office for more. This time around, the order of business is personal contact, either on the phone with other branch stables (if the trainer is one of those who has his headquarters and hindquarters in more than one place) or with the owners of his horses.

One of those phone calls, so the story goes, went from trainer Laz Barrera to the owners of one of the horses in his stable to tell him that his horse "had died." "That's alright," replied the owner on the other end of the phone, "we'll get 'em next race." "No . . . no . . . no, you don't understand," Barrera said, raising his voice to impress upon the owner the urgency of the situation. "He *died!!!* . . . And I need $800 to cart his body away."

Most owners who visit the stable—that is, if they can get their cars or chauffeur-driven limos past the Pinkerton guards at the gate—come primarily to see their horses. The pedigreed ones come just to visit, inquire about their horses' health, and maybe give their horse a pat and a little treat. Others, who wouldn't eat ladyfingers unless they were manicured, believe their horse is Secretariat in drag; and although the horse obviously is not, the owners view all such great truths as blasphemous, demanding their horse win, and constantly carp and criticize. Still others give suggestions for the running of their horse with all the solemnity of Moses delivering his tablets from the Mount, overriding their trainer's instructions.

There are times those suggestions are well-received or, at least, taken into consideration by the trainer. LeRoy Jolley, the trainer of Genuine Risk, was from the old school, a Kentuckian with old-time Southern standards, one of which was that males were males and females were, well, different, and that Genuine Risk, being a filly, would not race against colts in the Derby. Jolley relented after owner Diana Firestone convinced him to train the horse nicknamed "Jenny" for the Derby, and Genuine Risk became only the second filly to win the Derby, in 1980. In 2001, Point Given was the Derby favorite, but got off to a slow start and finished a disappointing fifth. Owner Prince Ahmed bin Salman took trainer Bob Baffert aside and suggested, ahem!, that Point Given go to the lead immediately; in both the Preakness and Belmont, the horse did, romping to powerful victories.

Somewhere in the midst of all this time juggling, about nine o'clock, the trainer must make his way over to the track for the early-morning workouts of his flock. Some prefer to be out on the track with their horses, watching them exercise or even ponying their own animals. Others will assume a vantage point, usually a trainer's stand set up by the track for such purposes, where the trainers can watch his—and other trainers'—horses, there to be joined by fellow members of his union. The scene is one of organized confusion, the track filled to the Plimsoll line with horses in all manner of motion, some leisurely moving with all the speed of the gestation period of the Galápagos turtle, others truant out on a romp, moving briskly but not urgently, and more than a few looking as if they were just stretching their legs in the morning air.

Then, suddenly, one of the horses will start like a warhorse at the sound of the bugle, burning up the track as the clocker, with stopwatch in hand, tries to record the time of the horse—that is, if he can pick him out from the rest without the aid of a Geiger counter, his mind numbing at the number of horses on the track. Some turtle along, their times such that they could be clocked by a sundial; others flash along the track, their feet ablur, registering fractions half as fast as Minute Rice. Trainer Jimmy Jones, watching his horse, Coaltown, once told a fellow trainer, "I'll tell you something, but if you tell anybody else, I'll say it's a lie. I worked that horse a half and he shaded :44. I can't believe my watch." As the horse finishes his split, or fraction of a mile, the clocker will call out his time for the trainer, usually in elliptical fashion, as "fifty-nine and two" for five-eighths, or somesuch, the trainer instinctively noting it as either too fast, too slow, or, like Baby Bear's porridge, just right.

Sometimes the routine workout is anything but. One workout morning, as Charlie Whittingham was leading Sunday Silence through the tunnel onto the track for a gallop, the colt became spooked by something or other and, rearing up, smote Whittingham's right temple with its left front hoof. As concerned stable-hands gathered around Whittingham, still clinging to Sunday Silence's shank, Whittingham cracked wise, "I just hope he didn't hurt his foot banging on my noggin that way."

Even though a horse runs against time—as in Colonel Bradley's age-old formula that a Derby winner is the horse who can run the last quarter in twenty-five seconds or less—he is also running against his competition. Every trainer has more than some concern that his horses may be morning glories, burning it up in the morning and dying in the afternoon when it's money time, unable to duplicate their workout performance in the heat of competition.

While the time is important—not only to the trainer but to others, like the early-morning bettors gathered at the rail and the next day's chart readers, as well as other trainers—the *who* riding him is equally important. If it's a jockey rather than an exercise rider on the horse, everyone snaps to attention. There must be a reason for this, so the reasoning goes, otherwise why would a jock be up on the horse? Most times it's to correct a horse's faults, like being afraid of the rail, or to acclimate a horse to a new jockey or new set of blinkers or other equipment changes, but it still could be to get the best time possible out of him. Who knows? That's part of the game.

Even as all of this is going on, another game is being played in the trainer's stand, the game of small talk, gossip, and rumor, as those gathered in close quarters retail extra large-size stories and pass along twice-told tales—some of them trains of thought that haven't quite reached their destination before they are picked up on. There are rumors that hadn't reached the paper yet, intelligence and information about other trainers' horses, hearsay about which trainer has approached another trainer's owner in an attempt to get him to move his horses to his stable, and various and sundry other bits of news—the dirt dished sounding like all of Solomon's wives had caught him out on the town with another woman. And then, of course, invariably there are conspiratorial whisperings, deals being made between trainers, horses to be bought and sold.

The definition of an *owner* is someone who has the right to say who can use a thing. And many trainers fall into that definition, owning a few, or a percentage of a few, of the horses in their stable. In smaller stables, it may be a goodly proportion of those in his barn; in some, all. Trainers come by their own horses either by purchasing them outright from other trainers or at sales or via the claiming route, as Howie Tescher did, almost breaking Joe DiMaggio's record by dropping a claim card into the Arlington Park box in nine straight races. Others, most notably trainers of larger stables, own their horses by virtue of breeding rights to a stud horse they once trained.

Then there's the story told by Joe Palmer of an owner who sold a horse to a trainer for $1,200, the horse and all the rest of the owner's horses running in his trainer's name because his heart specialist told him he was going to have to take it easy and avoid excitement, which included drinking, smoking, and horse racing. So, to tip-toe around the doctor's advice, the owner was running all his horses in his trainer's name.

There are times when a trainer, if not acting *as* an owner, is acting *for* an owner, one with pockets so deep he has to have them let out by his tailor. In return, the successful trainer-cum-sales agent receives either a commission, a percentage of the horse, or the horse itself to train. Some of those trainers, like Bob Baffert, have the ear of wealthy patrons who believe in his judgment and give him the money to buy stock far beyond what his bankroll

Top Winning Trainers in One Year (Based on 100 Wins)		
Name	Wins	Year
William Molter	136	1954
	142	1956
Frank Martin	166	1974
Jack Van Berg	496	1976
Lazaro Barrera	127	1977
	100	1978
D. Wayne Lukas	131	1984
	218	1985
	259	1986
	343	1987
	318	1988
	305	1989
	267	1990
	289	1991
	230	1992
	147	1994
	194	1995
	192	1996
	169	1997
Bob Baffert	139	1998
	169	1999
	146	2000
	138	2001
Bobby Frankel	117	2002

will allow—as Prince Ahmed bin Salman did, pointing Baffert in the direction of War Emblem a scant eleven days before the 2001 Derby, and underwriting the purchase of 90 percent of the potential winner for $900,000.

Trainers with big-money clients may spend as much as half their time servicing those big-money clients, advising and scouting for them and assisting them at private sales and haunting sales pavilions in search of potential new stock. Recently, trainer Nick Zito, on behalf of one of his well-heeled clients, offered a million bucks to purchase a lightly raced colt named Senor Swinger, saying only: "A year ago, who'd heard of a couple of colts named Medaglia d'Oro and War Emblem?" And trainers Bob Baffert and Joe Orseno were busy at the same auction offering up money in the same neighborhood for their owners for a three-year-old son of El Prado.

One of Fitzsimmons's chores for Belair was to inspect the new crop of colts each year. One year, leaning on a fence and taking a gander at the new yearlings, he espied one that Mr. Woodward had taken a fancy to, a blaze-faced colt out of Sir Galahad III. Asked by Woodward what he thought about the little one out of the great sire, Fitz only had eyes for the colt's nose and said something to the effect, "The nostrils are a little small for my tastes. They have trouble breathin' during a race if the nostrils ain't big enough . . . we'll just have to take 'em and see what we can do." What he did was make a Triple Crown winner of "'em," Gallant Fox.

Sometimes a trainer's loyalty is split. Take the rumor that Baffert wanted to keep Bob and Beverly Lewis's colt Silver Charm, not yet a Derby winner, in his stable so badly that when rival trainer D. Wayne Lukas began casting covetous eyes in Charm's direction for one of his clients, willing to pay a multiple of Charm's purchase price pending a workout preview, Baffert not only instructed his exercise rider to work the horse slow but also to make sure that he could be heard saying, "The Charm felt kind of stiff today."

Now, with most of his morning's work behind him, all that remains is the final-final preparations for that day's races. And some final decisions, such as should his horse wear blinders, or "blinkers," those leather flaps attached to a horse's bridle to curtail side vision called "eye shields" by sportswriter Jimmy Cannon, who said of them: "They're put on horses so they won't be frightened by getting a look at the horse players who bet on them." For horses easily disturbed or distracted, blinkers may be the answer.

After a few more matters to be attended to, including putting on a lucky tie or jacket, the trainer goes off to the paddock area, there to perform the last-minute duties of a trainer: lifting his jockey aboard his mount at the cry of "Riders up!" and adding a few clipped words to his already-given instructions, delivered in words as succinct as a Western Union telegram, then expressing a few final words, part benediction, part well-wishes, in English or Spanish or whatever is appropriate—such as Lucien Laurin, in French, telling his jock, "Use *ton propre jugement*"—before departing the scene to take his vantage point for the race.

The trainer repeats this ritual over and over again, for as many times as he has horses in races that day, then goes to the vantage point to watch the races and, after a full day, goes home. Only to start all over again the next A.M.

While D. Wayne Lukas says, "The negatives will eat you alive . . . ," every trainer worth his stable is looking for the positive things, the things that are more than just the 10 percent of the purse, that once motivated trainer John E. Madden to say, "I would sooner train a good horse than be president of the United States," and trainer James Rowe Sr., to request his epitaph read nothing more than HE TRAINED COLIN, the great undefeated horse of the early twentieth century.

What could be more rewarding than sitting by the owner on Derby Day, as trainer Carl Nafzger did on that first Saturday in May 1990, and describing Unbridled's drive to the wire to ninety-two year-old Frances Genter: "He's taken the lead, Mrs. Genter. . . . He's gonna win! . . . He's a winner, Mrs. Genter, he won it, he won it! You won the Kentucky Derby, Mrs. Genter. . . ."

Trainer Charlie Whittingham once said: "If you go anywhere in American and they find out you're a horse trainer, the only thing they ever ask you is 'You ever win the Kentucky Derby?'" Charlie Whittingham did, with Ferdinand and Sunday Silence. Carl Nafzger did. And so, too, did many others, all celebrities in the world of trainerdom—and the goal of trainers everywhere.

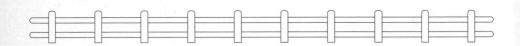

Three great jockeys of the twentieth century: Ted Atkinson, Earl Sande, Eddie Arcaro
(Copyright © Hulton Archive).

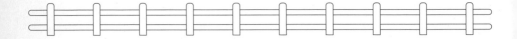

4

THE JOCKEYS

I n the words of the late, great Pulitzer Prize–winning sports-writer Jim Murray, "You have to be half-man, half-animal to be a jockey. You have to, in a sense, be able to think like a horse. You have to sense his mood, gauge his courage, cajole him into giving his best."

Sunny Jim Fitzsimmons had once advanced the trainer's defi-nition: "A good jock does not impede the animal," implying that the horse makes the rider. However, that begets a discussion with two sides and no end. It's much like the story about the wives of composer Jerome Kern and lyricist Oscar Hammerstein II (who collaborated on *Show Boat*). A fan approached the two women at a party and told Mrs. Kern how much she admired Mr. Kern for writing the show's famous song "Ol' Man River." Whereupon Mrs. Hammerstein interjected, "*Her* husband wrote 'Da, da, da-dum.' *My* husband wrote 'Ol' Man River'." It is the jock who writes "Da, da, da-dum . . ." to the words provided by the horse.

From the lowliest of the low bull rings at state fairs to the high-est of high-priced races, a good jock is one who fits his mount like a well-suited saddle, can handle him with the sensitive touch of a piano tuner with reckless disregard for life and limb, and is able to control a half ton of raging horseflesh, all in the name of booting his horse home a winner.

That delicate fusion of man and horse can be seen in the likes of nineteenth-century great Isaac Murphy, who staked more claims to records than an Alaskan claim jumper, winning 44 percent of his races. Or, more recently, Willie Shoemaker, who, winning with a dismal monotony and startling variety, found his way into the winner's circle one out of every five of his rides. And, along the way, Eddie Arcaro, called by *Sports Illustrated* "the most

ALL-TIME LEADING JOCKEYS 6000+ WINS		
Jockey	Career Years	Wins
*1. Lafitt Pincay Jr.	37	9,275
2. Bill Shoemaker	42	8,833
*3. Pat Day	30	8,000
4. Russell Baze	29	8,000
5. David Gall	43	7,396
6. Chris McCarron	29	7,139
7. Angel Cordero Jr.	35	7,057
8. Jorge Velasquez	33	6,795
9. Sandy Hawley	31	6,449
10. Larry Snyder	35	6,388
11. Eddie Delahoussaye	32	6,380
12. Carl Gambordella	38	6,349
13. Earlie Fires	35	6,105
14. John Longden	41	6,032

Data source: Top Jockeys—2001 ESPN Almanac.
*Active.

famous man to ride a horse since Paul Revere," finishing in the money on more than half the 24,000 horses he rode.

Down through racing's long corridors, the names of horses and their jockeys have become as linked as Alexander the Great and his horse Bucephalus, the duke of Wellington and his horse Copenhagen, and Roy Rogers and his horse Trigger. Together, passenger and carrier are viewed as one—as Arcaro and Whirlaway and Citation, Earl Sande and Gallant Fox, Johnny Longdon and Count Fleet, Ron Turcotte and Secretariat, Steve Cauthen and Affirmed, and on and on. For, practically, you can't have one without the other and, in reality, you can't imagine one without the other.

And so it is, in a field for fashioning nimbuses, that the names of the jockeys are as famous as those of the horses they rode in on—names like Tod Sloan, Snapper Garrison, Isaac Murphy, James McLaughlin, Jimmy Winkfield, James Butwell, Willie Knapp, Johnny Loftus, Buddy Ensor, Earl Sande, George Woolf, Sonny Workman, Johnny Longdon, Eddie Arcaro, Eric Guerin, Conn McCreary, Willie Shoemaker, Bill Hartack, Walter Blum, Pat Day, Chris McCarron, Gary Stevens, Ted Atkinson, Jerry Bailey, Lafitt Pincay Jr., and all the other greats who stand taller in racing history than they ever stood in their stirrups.

The first of racing's legendary jockeys was Tod Sloan, a dwarf of a man who would get lost in a crowd of two, weighing all of 91 pounds, and standing, as they said in the press of the day, "knee-high to a grasshopper"—that day being the last decade of the nineteenth century. Having won everything but the America's Cup in the United States, Sloan went voyaging over to England to challenge the best the English racing world had to offer.

For over two hundred years, the English had had their own system of riding, a system they were proud of, with jockeys, mostly from Newmarket, learning to ride under the tutelage of regular trainers. And, for those two hundred years, the long line of Newmarket trainers had their own idea of just how a horse should be ridden. Partial to a single orthodoxy, they taught their jocks to ride stiff and upper, like their lips, their heads held so high they had a double chin in the backs of their necks. They pointed with justifiable pride to Fred Archer, one of their pupils, who, in 1885, had ridden 246 winners, and to others like Wood, Watts, Barrett, Loates, Robinson, and Cannon, as jockeys who had come under their system of training and all of whom became winners, riding, as they did, "straight up in the air," as it was called.

Came now Sloan, who brought over his own system, that of crouching forward in the saddle with his head bent over his horse's withers, his entire body resting on its neck and shoulders, leaning into his run and buffeting the wind with his collarbone, making for less wind resistance. The English called him a monkey and made fun of his style, but his "monkey on a stick" style and shortened stirrups not only won for him many a classic (or, as they say over there, "group" races), but also the envy and hatred of many an English bookmaker and owner.

It was while he was in England, enjoying success after success, becoming toasted, and egg'd and kippered and coffee'd or tea'd, that W. C. Whitney went to the expense of bringing Sloan back over to ride his horse, Ballyhoo Bey, in the Futurity of 1900 at Sheepshead Bay, New York. Sloan's contract called for the then unheard-of fee of $5,000 for one race, his transportation to and from England, and all expenses—not an insignificant item, since Sloan, who had been hobnobbing with nobility on the other side of the pond, including his good friend the Prince of Wales, later King Edward VII, was used to living royally, employing the services of a valet and requiring a score of trunks to house his resplendent wardrobe.

Having ridden Ballyhoo Bey in a workout, and proclaiming "He's the best horse I ever threw a leg over," the little jockey rode him to a length-and-a-half victory in the Futurity, beating three horses carrying the colors of Whitney's hated rival, Foxhall Keene. Instantly, Keene filed a protest on the grounds that Sloan had allowed Ballyhoo Bey to bump one of the Keene colts. And, though the protest was disallowed, Whitney never forgave the accusation, donating his Futurity winnings to a Boston hospital and vowing never to look at a race of any kind if his horses were running against those of the Keenes.

For his part, Foxhall Keene, a member of the English Jockey Club, never forgave Sloan, and promised to get even. And so it was that, after Sloan returned to England and his winning ways, Keene's emnity lathered over, and he initiated charges that Sloan had bet heavily on his own mounts, jockeys then being prohibited from betting in England. Sloan paid the supreme price for his perceived insolence in beating Keene's horses by being barred from racing in England for two years.

Sloan's banishment and ultimate reinstatement became the theme of George M. Cohan's 1904 play *Little Johnny Jones*, in which Cohan, as the jockey Johnny Jones, sings an updated version of "Yankee Doodle Dandy" ("Yankee Doodle came to London/just to ride the ponies/I am that Yankee Doodle Boy"), which became the title of the 1942 movie starring James Cagney in his Academy Award-winning performance.

Of such stuff are legends made.

Other jockeys have become as famous for their styles as Sloan was for his. In the long ago, Isaac Murphy was known for his cardiac-arrest whirlwind finishes, so much so that they exhausted horse and owner alike. Snapper Garrison likewise, his come-from-behind finishes immortalized in the phrase "Garrison finish." Then, there is Pat Day, who is a rider in the old classic style, once described as a cigar-store Indian because of the way he sits on a horse. Johnny Longdon was known for his push-me-pull-you style with the reins, which earned for him the nickname "the Pumper." And Eddie Arcaro rode with his hands close together on the horses' manes, as opposed to the wide cross employed by most.

Then there are the credentialed members of the "whistle-while-you-work" group, singing, chirping, and talking to soothe their savage beasts, the foremost of which was Angel Cordero Jr. Once, after finding out that Bold Forbes had been trained in Puerto Rico and only understood Spanish, Cordero could be heard singing out to him, "New shoes, babee, Papa gonna get you new shoes" in Spanish, as he booted him home a winner time and again.

Snapper Garrison, Christian name Edward, was also known for something else: his one-upsmanship, especially at the start of a race. In days of yore, before the mechanical starting gate was adopted in the 1930s, unsure starts were all but guaranteed, with starters initiating the beginning of a race either by the beating of a drum or, more often, the waving of a red flag.

Garrison was able to use the starter and the starting line to his advantage, as he did at the World's Fair American Derby in 1893. Gingerly maneuvering his mount, Boundless, into position, Garrison caught the eye of the starter and, touching his cap, asked leave to dismount. "What's up?" asked the starter, a man named Pettingill, and known as "Pet." "My saddle girth has come loose," replied Garrison, "Well, then, dismount and fix it quickly," said Pet. And so, the jock they called "Snapper" dismounted and called his valet out onto the track to help him. Between the two, they fiddled and played around with the saddle girth while the rest of the field stood at the line, tensed and ready to go—or, as they say

Kent Desormeaux attains every jockey's goal as he rides Fusaichi Pegasus to win the 2000 Kentucky Derby *(Copyright © Getty Images, Getty Images North America)*.

in trackspeak, "chomping at the bit." Someone estimated the time Garrison spent "fixing" his saddle girth as being in the neighborhood of one hour and fifty-two minutes, not only giving gamblers in poolrooms and in the betting rings more time to make their bets, but also wearying the other horses as they fretted around the starting line, carrying their weight. When the flag, finally, fell, it was Garrison on his horse Boundless who was boundless in energy, while the others were so tired and drained from the wait they looked like they were reacting at the pace of a responsive reading. Garrison and Boundless breezed to an easy victory.

Starters were an important part of racing back then, many of the starters becoming celebrities in their own right. One of the most famous was Colonel Jack Chinn, whose patter at the starting gate was once recorded by sportswriter Al Spink and went something like this:

> You, Isaac Murphy, you take that dog back and keep him back. John Harper told me you were a gentleman. You are acting today, suh, like a highwayman. You are trying to steal this race before it's fairly started, suh. You, Thorpe, cut out them monkey shines. Walk that jennie of yours up to the gate, stand thar and behave yourself, suh. If you don't it will cost you more money than you can earn in a thousand years, suh. You, Van Dusen, you, suh, you reptile, you're never happy 'cept when you're trying to make all hands miserable. Get to the far side and stay thar or I'll have to slash your crazy head off. Now, Overton, steady your hoss and come up slower in the center. Now you, Mooney, come next to the Monk, nicely, gently and easily. Come on over here, Garrison. You, Snapper, come quick or I'll go git you. That's it. . . . We'll start this race right, an even break for all, or we'll stay here till tomorrow mawnin'. A square deal for all, a square deal or the blanket comes right off your hoss. . . .

On and on it went until, finally, Chinn was able to say, "Oh, at last you all believe me, and you're all comin' my way like little gentlemen. Come on then . . . come on . . ." and with the drop of the flag, away they went.

Not every start was as well-organized or orderly as those conducted by Colonel Chinn, it having been said by some who were at Saratoga that fateful day in 1919 when Man o' War lost the only race of his career, that it wasn't so much Upset who beat him nor his being blocked out on the rail as many thought, but that the substitute starter that day dropped his flag when the horse called "The Mostest" was facing the wrong way.

Other times, the starters somehow, someway, got involved in the race itself, not just the start. Take Jake Beckley, then one of the National League's leading batsmen, who supplemented his income by working winters as a starter at racetracks in California and New

Orleans. One winter, Jake was working at an Oakland racetrack. His friends always knew which horse Jake had bet on by which horse in the field got the heaviest whack from the whip he carried to spur him on, just as the flag fell. On one occasion, with Jake having put his wad on the favorite in the race, he couldn't resist the temptation to give the horse of his choice a parting sting to ensure his getting a jump on the field. However, the lash of the long, snakelike whip caught up in the horse's tail and, winding itself into a tangle, hung there. For a mile the favorite dragged that six pounds of extra weight but, finally, the drag became too much, and it finished second by a neck. From that day on, Beckley keep his whip lashed to his wrist.

The starter is now long gone, replaced by a mechanized gate that springs open to simultaneously release the horses at the same second. But, as with all advancements made in the name of progress, it has also replaced the characters and the stories that went with the old.

Most jocks come up the hard way. Eddie Arcaro started at the age of thirteen galloping horses at fifty cents a romp, usually on credit. After months and months of wageless and thankless service, and more than a few taunts from trainers that he would never become a rider, the youngster left Latonia Racetrack near his hometown of Cincinnati and took off for California, where a gypsy trainer gave him his first chance. But his first win was unforthcoming. In fact, in stories lengthening like Pinocchio's nose—which is only fair, considering the size of Arcaro's, which earned him the nickname "Banana Nose"—his first 45 or 100 or 250 starts, depending upon who was telling the story, were unforthcoming. Willie Shoemaker's start was equally disheartening. Taking up racing at the age of sixteen, this mere bat-eared wisp of a lad, standing just four feet eleven inches in his size one-and-a-half boots, was, as his employer in California told him, destined never to be a rider. And turned loose by the trainer who kept another exercise boy he thought more promising.

Becoming a full-fledged jockey is a survivor sport in and of itself. For, in order to make it as an accredited jockey, the wannabe must survive a series of hurdles, the first of which is attending a jockey school, where he is given his jockey's test, which consists of breaking from the starting gate and running in the company of other horses for a given distance, usually an eighth of a mile. Upon graduation, he receives an exercise rider's license allowing him to exercise horses for any trainer willing to give him mounts. Then, upon formal recommendation or sponsorship from a trainer, the jockey-to-be can apply for an apprentice riding license which, once secured, qualifies him as an apprentice jockey, the lowest rung on the jockey's career ladder. Now called a "bugboy"—a designation that, according to famed writer A. J. Liebling, was originated by a Colonel Stingo in the long, long ago when, abandoning the program's main text, he began doodling in the margins marking his program with two asterisks or "bugs" next to a jockey's name "to indicate that he is an apprentice, one of small experience, a neophyte"—he receives a ten-pound weight allowance on his mounts until he wins five races and, thereafter, receives a single bug, or five-pound allowance, for the remainder of his first full calendar year of racing.

However, while apprentice jockeys may be second-class citizens in the jockey colony, they may become first-class citizens in the racing community, as witnessed by Shoemaker, who, his face still a stranger to the razor, rode 219 winners, second highest in the nation, in his apprentice year.

The jockey is, generally speaking, an independent contractor. Thus, his services are for hire, either as a day rider, a substitute, or, in the case of leading jocks, under contract to a specific owner.

The most preferable arrangement is, as one of the first jockeys to have such an arrangement, Tod Sloan, called it, being "contractually obligated" to an owner. And while not a "'til obituary notices do we part" type of arrangement—Eddie Arcaro having jumped from Calumet Farms to Greentree Stables—it normally guarantees the jockey a certain sum and quality mounts that may bring him more. One of those who was offered such an arrangement in the long ago, Earl Sande, turned down a flat fee of $10,000 to ride Gallant Fox for a year, instead opting for a percentage of all the purses he won, a percentage he earned by riding The Fox to the 1930 Triple Crown—along with immortality, becoming the subject of a poem by Damon Runyon which ended: "Why it's that Handy Guy Named Sande, Bootin' them Babies in."

The substitute jocks are represented by an agent whose sole purpose in life is obtaining rides for his clients. Limited to the number of clients he can handle—no more than one journeyman and two apprentices—the jockey's agent hustles for his clients, for a fee, of course, the tariff usually being between 25 percent and 30 percent of his client's winnings. Bearing a dogeared copy of *Condition Book*, which he studies the way a little boy studies the entrails of a toy he has just taken apart, to see what races and places his clients might best fit, the agent will pursue trainers to get them mounts, telling the trainer that the jockey in question is a good gate, or whip, rider, or whatever it is he thinks the trainer is looking for, while his client jockeys sit around like numbers at a meat market, ready to take their turn.

And woe betide the poor jock who is injured or not performing to form, for the agent circles the trainer like the proverbial shark smelling blood, trying to get the trainer to swap jockeys in midstream. Substitute jocks not only have a place in racing history but, many times, have made history themselves, as Eddie Arcaro did taking the place of Albert Snider aboard Citation in his Triple Crown year of 1948, after Snider mysteriously disappeared in the Florida Keys; as George Woolf did aboard Seabiscuit for his famous match race against War Admiral, after The Biscuit's regular jock, Red Pollard, was injured; or as Braulio Baeza did, riding Arts and Letters in the '69 Derby after a spooked horse fell on Bill Hartack and scratched him from the race, prompting *Sports Illustrated* to write: "It's not every Derby that trainer can lose his rider and come up with a Baeza as a substitute."

Every jock worthy of his silks will admit that one of his primary concerns is weight. Already thin as a whisper, their career weighs in the balance if the scales in the scaleroom register more than 110 pounds, give or take a pound or two, which, when combined with a saddle, two to four pounds of clothing (and more in cold climes), and a flak jacket will bring the total weight the horse will carry up into the teens. Anything more, and they not only jeopardize their chances of winning, but their careers.

A wise man once wrote the following, in a piece of Ogden Nash-like wisdom:

> Bill Bounce, being fat for a jockey,
> Tried steaming to make him less stocky.
> They treated him so
> That he had to eat snow,
> And change his profession to hockey.

And, while no jock wishes to change his profession to hockey, or anything else for that matter—Eddie Arcaro, when asked why he had become a jockey, said, "Because I'd be just another little guy waiting for a table in a restaurant"—they know that to maintain their career as a jockey means they have to maintain their weight. Which means that, for some, it's a daily visit to the steamroom before they check into the scaleroom to be weighed in before the day's races. Others undergo a dietary straitjacket. And still, a few resort to taking weight-reducing drugs or supplements, which, in the case of Chris Antley, led to a dependency on drugs and, ultimately, his death.

Then there are some like Bill Hartack, who, after weighing his options, decided it would be better to switch than fight. Hartack took his tack and flew off to Hong Kong, where the weight allowances were more liberal and, riding the Hong Kong circuit for five years, there amassed a record of 72 wins in 686 mounts.

Over the years, the constituency of the jockey colony has changed many times over. Whereas today you can count the African-American jocks on someone's missing finger, there was a time when they were the dominant reinsmen on American tracks, winning fifteen of the first twenty-eight runnings of the Derby. In fact, fourteen of the fifteen jockeys in that first edition in 1875 were African-Americans. And their names, many of which have been lost to memory and history alike, were the biggest names in racing at the time; names like Isaac Murphy, Jimmy Winkfield, Willie Simms, Monk Overton, Alonzo Clayton, Erskine Henderson, and many, many more, too numerous to mention.

A highly racist, grudgingly complimentary article in the *New York Herald* of September 20, 1889, under the headline COLORED JOCKEYS SHOW THE WAY, told of their total dominance at Brooklyn's Gravesend Race Track: "If a composite photograph had been made of the jockeys who rode the six winners at Gravesend, it would have been as black as Erebus. There wouldn't have been a single light line in it, unless the camera had happened to catch Hamilton with his mouth wide open displaying the pearly white teeth which form the only relieving feature of his coal black face." The Hamilton referred to was Tony Hamilton, who, along with Isaac Murphy, Pike Barnes, Spider Anderson, and Isaac Lewis, had brought his horses home first or second in every race that afternoon.

However, all that changed in the first decade of the twentieth century when, as rumor had it, August Belmont, more than somewhat upset at the daredeviltry of Winkfield in making the jockeys

AFRICAN-AMERICAN JOCKEYS
KENTUCKY DERBY
1875–1903

Jockey	Year/Horse	Finish
Alonso Clayton	1892/Azar	1st
	1893/Plutus	2nd
	1895/Laureate	3rd
	1897/Ornament	2nd
Erskine Henderson	1882/Pat Malloy	9th
	1883/Chatter	7th
	1885/Joe Cotton	1st
Babe Hurd	1882/Apollo	1st
George G. Lewis	1880/Fonso	1st
Isaac Lewis	1886/Grimaldi	6th
	1887/Montrose	1st
	1888/The Chevalier	5th
	1889/Sportsman	6th
Oliver Lewis	1875/Aristides	1st
Isaac Murphy	1877/Vera Cruz	4th
	1879/Falsetto	2nd
	1880/Bancroft	3rd
	1884/Buchanan	1st
	1886/Lijero	5th
	1887/Pendennios	4th
	1889/Once Again	7th
	1890/Riley	1st
	1891/Kingman	1st
	1893/Mirage	5th
James "Soup" Perkins	1895/Halma	1st
Willie Simms	1896/Ben Brush	1st
	1898/Plaudit	1st

Data source: Kentucky Derby Media Guide, 1997.

(CONTINUED)		
Jockey	Year/Horse	Finish
William Walker	1875/Bob Wolley	4th
	1876/Bombay	8th
	1877/Baden-Baden	1st
	1896/The Winner	7th
Jimmy Winkfield	1900/Thrive	3rd
	1901/His Eminence	1st
	1902/Alan-a-Dale	1st
	1903/Early	2nd

riding his horses look like life's losing stuntmen, banned Winkfield from his track. Other track owners followed suit, banning Winkfield and all African-Americans from theirs. Thus ended the golden age of African-American jockeys, another not taking the reins on a major track until the 1990s, and not in the Derby until 2000, when Marlon St. Julien became the first African-American in eighty years to ride in that classic.

Another change in the makeup of the jockey colony has been the addition of Latino jockeys. However, its start was, at best, only a token one, with Joseph Rodriguez riding Upset in the 1920 Derby, and Manny Gonzalez up on Burnt Cork in the '43 edition. Still, their incorporation into the fraternal order of jockeys fell somewhere below registration on the radar screen, one would-be jockey, Ralph Neves, complaining, "It is crazy . . . they name the race tracks, the biggest races, and the cities here with Spanish names, but they won't let us ride." Then, in the 1950s, Latino jockeys began to get mounts and, what started as a trickle with Hank Moreno riding Dark Star to victory in the '53 Derby, became, by the late '80s, a Niagara, as more and more Latinos joined the passing post parade, the most prominent of whom were Angel Cordero Jr., Braulio Baeza, and Lafitt Pincay Jr.

Those ancient and honorable romantics who long ago committed themselves to the quaint notion that jockeying was a for-men-only vocation and that women need not apply, thank you!, were in for a rude awakening from their outdated dream in 1969, for that was the year women first entered the ranks of the previously all-male contingent of jockeys. The first woman to pass her jockey's test and be issued a license to ride was Barbara Jo Rubin. However, instead of welcoming her to their fraternity of saddles, the male jockeys at Tropical Park found her presence a burr under theirs and threatened to strike, forcing the owner of her mount to cave in and announce that she would not ride in her

ALL-TIME LEADING FEMALE JOCKEYS
Julie Krone
Patricia Coosey
Diane Crump
Rosemarie Homiester
Diane Nelson
Cindy Knoll
Patty Barton
Donna Barton-Brothers
Robyn Smith
Cheryl White
Mary Dosier
Patti Brothers

Data source: About.com/sports/horseracing.

scheduled debut. While both sides issued legal threats and the jockeys were fined $100 each for their actions, another woman, Diane Crump, received permission to ride and became, on February 7, 1969, the first woman to ride into history, adding yet another word to the congress of riders: *jockette*. After Crump took the lead, others, like Hall of Famer Julie Krone, the first female to win a Triple Crown event, the 1993 Belmont, and Patricia Cooksey, the only woman besides Krone to ride more than 2,000 winners, followed in her tracks, making the field of jockeys a full-fledged coed colony.

There are few moments in sports to rival the excitement seconds before the horses enter the starting gate. The horses have come through the tunnel out of the paddock area onto the track, one by one, and, after first wandering around like little ducklings, form into a parade in the order of their post positions. Some of the horses preen, almost as if they were saving themselves and didn't want to turn a hair if they could help it; others, fractious and frisky, tug at the reins, sometimes to be rounded up by outriders and brought back into line. The jocks, bedecked in silks of many colors—the very term "silks" a misnomer, like Panama hats, which are made in Ecuador, silks having been replaced by modern, more easily cleanable synthetic fabrics, like nylon and Lycra—after first riding their horses up the track away from the gate, now reverse themselves and lead their mounts back.

The jockeys now guide their mounts toward the starting gate, there to be loaded into their individual stalls in the order of their post positions. But going in is not the same discipline for all horses. Most go in without any prodding; but then there are the dwellers, the refusers, the balkers, and the fractious. For them, the starter has all manner of equipment to ensure that they're loaded in and ready to run when the gate springs open, including a ten-foot lead-in strap, which is hooked to the horse's halter to enable the crew to lead the balky horse into the gate; a buggy whip, which is snapped behind a recalcitrant to make him move forward; a set of nose tongs, to hold the horse's head in a still position, pointed forward, which come out when the horse takes off; and even a flipping harness, which prevents a horse from turning around or even lying down.

Which is not to say that starting gates are foolproof, as witnessed by a race at the Atlantic City Race Track back in 1974. For on that August day, Basic Witness, the favorite in the Longport Handicap stakes race, sat in the starting gate with Carlos Barrera ready in the saddle as the back stall door closed behind him. And then the gates swung open and they were "Off!" That is, all but Basic Witness, who, as the other horses broke cleanly, stayed in his stall doing his best impression of a statue. Barrera gave him a kick, then a whack with his whip, but all Basic Witness did was paw at the ground. Seems that his tail was caught in the rear of the gate. The track steward, Sam Boulmetis, could only shake his head and say, "At first, we thought the horse just refused to run. Then we thought there was a tailing problem. Some horses will rear up in the starting gate, so a helper will stand in back, on top of the gate, and hold the horse's tail up. This is called 'tailing,' and it usually keeps the horse from rearing up." Then he added, "We figured someone was tailing Basic Witness and forgot to let go, but the film didn't show anyone behind the horse . . . We determined that somehow he got his tail caught just as they were closing the back stall door." Thankful Basic Witness didn't, in the words of Boulmetis, "break real hard or he would have lost his tail," the track refunded the money bet on the favorite.

Assured that all of the horses are in, their heads forward and ready to run, the starter hits the button, the gates spring open . . . and *THEY'RE OFF!!!*

The dean of early-twentieth-century sportswriters, Grantland Rice, in the purplish style of his day, once wrote: "Did you ever notice, old pal, in the race track's dizzy spin, there are ninety ways that a horse can lose—with only one to win?"

Sometimes, the losing is done long before the horses even reach the starting gate, back in the paddock area where the horse is prepared for the race, with the equipment. It is there, after the jockeys have been boosted up onto their mounts—the thorough-bred being a high-strung animal, may rebel at a sudden tug on the stirrups—that the jocks begin to touch-feel their saddle, their girth, their reins, their everything. For, more than once, has the equipment failed as much as the horse or jockey, Walter Blum once having had a saddle slip during a race, had to hang on for dear life, and Jorge Velasquez likewise after finding out his horse did not have a steel bit at the end of his reins.

And, if the great god Pluvius is up in his heavenly seat raining down on the track, whether in a steady drizzle on an unlimited run or in raindrops as far apart as currants in a cake at a church bake sale, or the track is a navigable stream with the consistency of gumbo and chances are that the jockeys at the finish will look like survivors from an explosion at a mud factory, a pair of gog-gles is the order of the day.

Losing may also come at the very start of the race, at the starting gate. Horses have stumbled coming out of the gate, as War Emblem did in the Belmont in 2002; hit the gate with their faces, as Seattle Slew did when the bell rang at the 1977 Derby; or been knocked to their knees by the opening cavalry charge out of the gate, as Brevity was at the 1936 Derby. Some superhorses recover; most don't.

As the horses come barreling out of the gate in a kamikaze dash with time too short for a course in etiquette, and each jockey's obvious disinclination to be left behind, the gathering storm takes on the looks of a demolition derby. One jock who was famous for his damn-the-torpedoes, full-speed-ahead moves from the start was Jimmy "Wink" Winkfield who, at Chicago's Hawthorne Racetrack back in 1898, in the bloodrush of just a few strides, burst forth like an erupting volcano and raced his horse out of the four hole and across the path of the inside three horses in an attempt to get to the rail, bowling over the other three like tenpins.

Such collisions can occur anywhere on the track, whether at the beginning, where a jockey's run for the rail may have the same effect as that of a three-alarmer in a fireworks factory, clearing out the place; or midrace, when a jockey—deciding that, like the Alaskan Sled Dog Syndrome, if you're not in the lead the scenery never changes—tries to make too much of a bad thing and, his timing off, bangs into other horses in his drive for the lead. Whenever it happens, the results can be dangerous.

The mental makeup of most jockeys is such that they can no more be melted than steel nor welded than ice. And yet, they are not oblivious to the everpresent danger that rides with them, knowing that their jockey's license came with a warning that more than rivals that found on cigarette packs: being a jockey may be injurious to your health.

Howard Cosell, who always sounded like he was pulling a haystack apart to expose a needle, once harrumphed: "Can you name any other sport where an ambulance is required to follow the athletes around their field of play?" For once, Mr. Cosell had statistics to support his beating on the eardrums, the 2000 Waller Study of 2,700 jockeys over three years finding "6,545 significant injuries. . . . Most of the back and chest injuries the result of being thrown from the horse."

Many wear their injuries less as a badge of courage than as a mark of their profession. Lafitt Pincay Jr., with more than 9,500 wins, can add eleven broken collarbones, ten broken ribs, two spinal fractures, two punctured lungs, and two broken thumbs to his Hall of Fame plaque. Ron Turcotte didn't get away so lucky, his career coming to an end in a 1978 spill at Belmont Park that paralyzed him from the waist down. Then there was Ralph Neves, who was riding in a race at Bay Meadows aboard a horse that tripped and threw him headfirst into the rail. The track doctor rushed to his side, but could find no pulse and, after trying to revive him, covered him with a sheet. The track announcer even declared Neves "deceased." But, miraculously, Neves got off the gurney at the hospital and came back to ride later that same day.

Nobody ever said jockeys were altar boys in search of a service. Before he began coining money off his mint performances, Eddie Arcaro was a rough and dangerous rider, always riding like he was an accident on its way to happening. With a fire in his soul and a style that saw him treating the rules in a cavalier manner, Arcaro was called by one Washington Park official "a kid who either had to be awfully lucky or get killed." An incident at Arlington Park best illustrated Arcaro's early hardbitten style. Finding himself on the rail, all but hidden from the judges, Arcaro expertly slid a foot out and held the leg of a rival jockey all the way to the finish line. When the stewards inquired of Arcaro whether he had interfered with the ride of his rival, Arcaro's answer was, "Not so you'd notice it." Another time, at Aqueduct,

Arcaro, sure another jockey had deliberately interfered with him, tried to drive him into the rail and knock him off his horse. When called upon by the stewards to explain his actions, Arcaro, growling and sounding like he had just swallowed something or other, told the authorities he was only sorry he hadn't thrown his tormentor into the infield. For that, Arcaro's license was revoked for a year.

Arcaro's dark deeds pale when compared to the stretch duel between Brokers Tip and Head Play in the 1933 Kentucky Derby. And between their jockeys, Don Meade and Herb Fisher. As the two horses came pounding down the Churchill Downs homestretch at forty miles per hour, the two Kentucky feudists, make horse racing a contact sport—not just between horses, but between jocks—with a deadly game of rock 'em, sock 'em jockeying, Fisher grabbing the shoulder of the bearing-in Meade and Meade, in return, pulling at Head Play's saddlecloth, causing the horse's left rein to go slack. On they rode, clinging together like two shipwrecked survivors riding with a trespassers-will-be-prosecuted mentality. Meade now switched his attention to Fisher's shoulder and threw in a flick of his whip for good measure. At the end of the black-and-blue stagger to victory, it was Brokers Tip by one flaring nostril over Head Play. Or so it seemed in those days before the photo-finish camera was in vogue.

Such councils of war were commonplace back then, before the stewards had film to review. And, although there are occasional infractions today, when the extremes of the moment move the rider to, shall we say, less break the rules than test their elasticity, out-and-out roughhousing seems to be a thing of a bygone era.

There are reasons other than collisions and roughhousings that might cause jockeys to be thrown from their horses. Sometimes, it's the horse itself that causes the fall, either because the horse stumbles and falls, or because it has suddenly taken umbrage at having someone on its back. Recently, a horse at Saratoga flung his jockey into the air like a balloon with the string suddenly coming unattached and romped out into a parking lot to frolic. The great horse Forego was one of those who resented having someone on him. Described by his groom as "the kind of horse that if he wants to go left and you want to go right, you go left," many's the time he just stared back at his jockey with a malevolent look as if to say, "You're here by my leave, so just sit back and don't bother me." Mounting their Lochnivar and going that somewhere it carried him can make the jockey feel like Sigmund Freud, when he was once asked where he was riding, and he replied, "Don't ask me, ask the horse." Many times, it's better not to ask.

A loss might result from a jock's inability to handle his horse, as was the case with Eric Guerin's losing ride aboard Native Dancer in the '53 Derby, about which one writer commented: "He took that colt everywhere on the track except the ladies' room."

Over and above the obvious ways a horse can lose—be they the horse itself deciding it had no interest in racing (or, as Red Smith said, find racing "a sinful occupation"), or suffering a race-ending injury, or faulty equipment, or a bumping-hyphen-collision, or roughhousing—there are several other ways, most not obvious, which lie with the jockey himself. It may be because the jockey continually looks back in search of other horses, like a harassed Sunday-school teacher expecting to be hit in the back of the head by a well-aimed spitball, losing sight of his goal, the finish line. Or it may be because of his placement on the track, whether, as author Dick Francis said, "surrendering the outside to no man," or caught up in an inescapable cul-de-sac between horses and unable to make his move. Or because he attempts his horse's stretch kick too early and is unable to make the soufflé rise a second time with another. Or a misjudgment in the jockey's timing, either by trying to thread a needle between two horses that doesn't exist or, showing an admixture of angels and fools, both rushing in and fearing to tread. Or hundreds of others.

Whatever the reason for the jockey's gaffe, it spells *L-O-S-S* for the horse.

Even the great ones can commit gaffes. Arcaro apologized for losing the 1955 Kentucky Derby aboard Nashua, saying he had paid too much attention to Summer Tan, who finished third, and not enough to Swaps, who won. But the mother of all such jockey mistakes may have been the one committed by Willie Shoemaker in the '57 Derby, in which he reaped a thorn, not a rose. Common wisdom would have it that after a couple of hundred recitals—or, in Shoemaker's case, thousands—an artist should develop a sensitivity to his surroundings. However, aboard Gallant Man in the '57 Derby, after having inched a nose in front of the frontrunning Iron Liege, Shoemaker inexplicably stood up in his stirrups and stopped riding about fifteen lengths from the wire. And even though he tried to push the toothpaste back into the tube, re-engaging Gallant Man's gears almost immediately, it was too late, losing to Iron Liege by a literal nose.

Asked how he could mistake the finish line, which one steward, shaking his head, said, "you can't miss the finish line at Churchill Downs . . . it looks like the Taj Mahal," Shoemaker, with unimpeachable courtesy, like a little boy explaining away a bad report card, admitted to suffering a sharp lack of awareness of its placement and misjudging it. Even though he was destined forever to wear that tin can tied to his tail, Shoemaker, characteristically, took it in stride, saying, "You can ask a hundred people, and ninety of them can tell you who lost that Derby, but they can't tell you who won."

Those very few jockeys who have successfully managed to be able to "be, half-animal" and "think like a horse" in spite of all the hurdles they have had to face along the way are those cheered at the beginning of their careers with hope, midway through with faith, and, at the end, with appreciation.

And that's what they're in it for. That, and 10 percent of the purse.

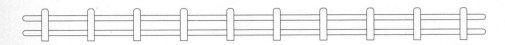

A bettor hoping "to catch financial lightening in a bottle" (Copyright © Hulton Archive).

5

THE BETTORS

Most bettors are sustained by the same kind of eternal hope that affects the orderers of celluloid teeth through the mails. Every day of the racing season, these movers of dreams dedicate themselves to the pursuit of feeding the mutuel machines in the hopes that they might be lucky enough to catch financial lightning in a bottle.

There must be something to this thing called luck. After all, how else to explain that, had it not been for a coin toss won by Lord Derby, the founder of the Epsom race, with a Sir Charles Bunbury back in 1780 to decide what to call the race, that race and all its namesakes would now be known as "the Bunbury," as in "the Kentucky Bunbury," instead of "Derby."

And so, every day, members of the turf-speculating populace, anxious to throw heads or tails with fortune, flock to the race-track of their choice, armed with the hope that Lady Luck will smile on them that day, plus more than a few analytical tools— from the *Daily Racing Form* to the everpresent tout sheets labeled *Clocker Somebodyorother*, and everything but a slide rule to extend their guesswork to the third place.

The first order of business for those found leaning against the pages of the *Racing Form* is to gulp down the big print, followed by a chaser of small type, comparing the well-balanced straight-edged numbers and unassailable figures of each horse to the morning line established by the track handicapper, figures that will last only until the first dollar hits the betting windows. To those entering the world of handicapping for the first time, those figures, which go under the names of past-performance charts, workout times, and chart notes, take on the look of hieroglyphics without subtitles. However, to the experienced dandruff scratcher, those figures, along with other approaches to handicapping, such as Beyer numbers and dosage factors, provide him with what he believes to be the mathematical wherewithal to pick winners out as easily as forking out the mushrooms on a $50 steak.

Some of the flood of figures confronting the reader can, however, be discounted at less than face value. The workout times, for instance. Only recently, *Washington Post* racing columnist and handicapping authority Andrew Beyer came across an instance in which an unraced three-year-old named Grand Hombre won a maiden race against a strong field at Gulfstream Park, winning the six-furlong race in 1:08-⅔, which, according to Beyer, was a "phenomenal time for any horse, let alone a first-time starter." And yet, Grand Hombre's workout times had been listed as being those of 53 seconds for ½ mile, another ½ in the same time, and a third in :54-⅗, times which, in the words of Beyer, "would barely get work pulling a Hansom cab in Central Park."

How, then, to explain the vast differential in the times between Grand Hombre's workout tabs and his race time? As Beyer explained it, Grand Hombre had been stabled at a private training center far from the eyes of clockers, where the trainer was responsible for reporting the horse's workout times. Add to that the fact that many trainers do not believe in having their horses burn up the track or burn themselves out going through fast workouts. Or, the trainer might even have misrepresented the horse's workout times in hopes of cashing a bet, a possibility Beyer dismissed in Grand Hombre's case.

Then, throw in Seattle Slew's very first workout, a five-furlong breeze on grass, which was recorded in the next day's *Racing Form* as being 1-⅖ instead of its clocked :58-⅖ and somehow credited by someone caught up in their mental underwear to "Seattle Sue" instead of Seattle Slew, and small wonder so many lay readers of the *Racing Form* feel they might have a better chance of deciphering the Rosetta Stone than the alien maze of figures confronting them.

Many, with eyes glazed at reading the unknowable in terms not worth knowing and suffering the pain of a coupon clipper's thumb running through the numbers, just chuck the charts and fall back on a preconceived set of standards known as "systems," of which there are many, ranging from old bromides like "a good horse can't be of a bad color" to betting the horse in the number-one position or the favorite to show, or any of a thousand-and-one others, most of them trains of thought that never quite reach their destinations.

Still others, chasing the mirage of vast riches bettors think are there for the taking, seek information or tips from any and all, despite all omens, silent writing on the wall and dire predictions about their fates, like the title of Damon Runyon's book *All Horse Players Die Broke.*

In search of information, even lightly circulated info heard through the grapevine, they take to wandering the grounds accepting it from anyone, much like the three horseplayers in the opening number of Runyon's *Guys and Dolls* who ". . . got the horse right here,/ The name is Paul Revere,/ And here's a guy that says if the weather's clear,/ Can do,/ Can do,/ This guy says the horse can do. . . ." Syd Thayer, who, more than a few years ago, had a summer job taking tickets at Old Keystone Park, remembers being asked by everyone who entered, "Got a tip for me today?" Thayer, almost as a mantra, would answer "seven in the fourth" as he tore their tickets in two. And, lo and behold, on those rare occasions when "seven in the fourth" would romp home a winner, those happy bettors who remembered from whence their tip had cometh would grease his hand with a dead president as thanks.

More than a few of those $2 bettors refer the matter to touts, those dishonest ventriloquists who deal out substantial slabs of silver lining at a price, looking to them like some mountaineer clinging to a jagged edge might greet a guide coming to haul him to safety. And then, feeding on their Delphic pronouncements like vegetarians on sweetbreads, carry their money and valise of hope forthwith to the betting windows.

And, then, there are those who have a hard time understanding the concept of alphabet soup, like the little old lady down at Hialeah a few years back who, according to Red Smith, asked a Pinkerton guard to explain the concept of the daily double. "Well, lady, it works like this," said the friendly guard. "You pick a horse, say the number five, in the first race, then you pick another, say number six, in the second. You bet on the two of 'em and it only costs two bucks. Well, if that number five loses in the first race, you're washed up, see? But if he wins, then you got a chance in the second to keep goin'. And if number six loses in the second, then you're washed up there, see? But if number five wins the first race and six cops the second, then you're filthy rich. See what I mean?" To which the little old lady said, "I think so. You mean I should bet number five in the first and number six in the second." "Christ no, lady," hurriedly said the Pinkerton, "I ain't touting. That was only an example. Ya gotta pick your own horses." "Well, thank you very much," said the L.O.L. (Little Old Lady), "I'm sure those two are very good horses," and away she went to the $2 window to buy a ticket on numbers five and six. Of course, they both came in, paying $1,186.40.

However the bettor arrived at his—or, in the case of L.O.L., her—decision, it's still a case of, as *Punch* magazine said back in 1845, "You pays your money and you takes your choice."

There was a time back yore—yore being the end of the nineteenth century and the beginning of the twentieth century—when betting rings run by bookmakers were the medium for betting on a race. Setting up shop near the paddock area or in the infield, those members of the so-called betting ring coined money so fast from an army of speculators that, sometimes, they had to have two men to tote up the swag, one to stuff the incoming money in a satchel and another, a figurator, who almost fractured his arm writing down the odds, either in a book or on a slate, all the while computing the odds as the bets came rolling in.

Most operated as pickpockets who let you use your own hands, the kind of men who, as proprietors of the men's room, would take the last towel just as their patrons reached for it, whether they needed it or no. One story of the time had it that Chris von der Ahe, then the owner of the St. Louis Browns, built what was called "a joke of a racetrack" around his ballpark and furnished the funds to back four or five books to take the gamblers' money. Most racetrack owners would have grown rich from such an arrangement, but von de Ahe lost money. One sharpie found out the reason. On every "sheet," as the record of bets made in each book was known, several large bets were always placed on the winning horses, past-posting them, all at the bottom of the page. What it meant was that the booking clerks had waited until the race was over, then put in some nice-sized bets on the winner for themselves. After he revealed the scheme to von der Ahe, von der Ahe waited until the day's races were over, then called his clerks into the office. "Poys," he said in his thick German accent, "I see vhere you haf been pudding down some nice pets for yourself on der puttom of der sheets. Now, poys, vot's done is done, vot's pet is pet, vot's gashed in is gashed in and vot you stole, you can't pay back, for you lost it back again. Bud," he warned, "from now on, poys, ve von't haf any lastdt pets on der sheets."

Rare indeed were the times when the skimmed milk of human kindness ran through the veins of the bookmakers. However, one time, a Chicago "penciler" was so inclined, and it redounded to his benefit, $3,000fold. Seems that the bookie had just finished putting up his figures on his slateboard when a little man barged through the crowd surrounding his ring, and, sticking a $20 bill under his nose, hollered, "Pass Book straight!" Although the bookie had chalked up odds amounting to 150-to-1 against Pass Book and stood to lose $3,000 if the horse won, he still looked at the $20 bill as his passport to dinner and loose cigar change. A few seconds later, he heard wrangling behind him, and, wheeling around, he saw the little man who had just bet the $20 being pushed by a big, raw-boned lady, obviously his wife, giving him whatfor, and telling him, in no uncertain terms to get that $20 bill off Pass Book. Her harangue went something like: "The very idea of you trying to squander our installment money on such a sausage as Pass Book . . . Why, the very idea! You go back to the man this very instant and tell him that I want that $20 bill put on the horse I told you to play, d'ye hear me???" And so, the little man slunk back to the bookie's stool and timidly began, "Say, old man . . ." Before he could continue, the bookie interrupted, "It's alright, mate. Give me your number and I'll erase the bet. What's the one she told you to play?" He entered the replacement bet and, about four minutes later, when Pass Book trotted home the winner, the bookie was $3,000 on the nice side of the ledger because he hadn't played it tough when the little man asked to change his bet.

These acts, however, were few and far between, most bookmakers were viewed as nothing short of burglars and highwaymen who, like highwaymen of old, made their clients "stand and deliver," having nothing to lose and making sure they didn't either.

And so it was, that, by the end of the first decade of the twentieth century, with reform agitation on the move, dedicated moralists in state after state promulgated legislation outlawing racetrack betting. And the day and age of betting rings became a part of racing's history, leaving behind only a few vestigial reminders of what once was in the terms of terms: *bookie* for a bookmaker's little book; *chalk* or *chalk players* for those who bet the favorites, their names erased and re-erased every time a bet was placed on them; and *scratch* for a line drawn on a slateboard for a horse that had been withdrawn from a race.

Also gone was racing itself, there not being enough customers interested in just coming out to the track for the sole purpose of "the improvement of the breed," as the defenders of the sports argued, without the additional divertisement of betting.

For almost a decade, racetracks remained closed with dire financial consequences not only to the sport itself—one breeder bluntly stating, "Unless a market can be found for the product by the opening of racing in some other section of the country, which does not seem likely, as the agitation at present is killing the game . . ."—but, also, to the economy of the states where the tracks had closed, one economist guesstimating that the closure of those in New York cost the state somewhere in the neighborhood of $26 million per year, including salaries lost, money spent at the tracks, and in the general area, including annual sale of yearlings, and so on.

To racing's rescue came a French import, the pari-mutuel system. Developed in the 1870s to thwart the rise of crooked bookmakers in Paris, the system was called *Paris Mutuels*—loosely translated to mean: "among ourselves, the Parisiennes"—and was designed to take the bookmakers out of the equation and put the track in their stead, acting as an intermediary for bettors who had bet against one another, not against the bookmakers.

In an effort to combat the growing wave of anti-gambling legislation that threatened the very existence of the sport, several American tracks, beginning with the New Orleans Fair Grounds in 1900 and Churchill Downs in 1908, introduced pari-mutuel wagering. With on-track betting replacing that previously conducted in betting rings and pool rooms, state legislatures agreed to legalize pari-mutuel wagering in exchange for a piece of the action.

That piece of the action, the states' cut, averaged approximately 16 percent. And, as one knowledgeable bettor groused, "Nobody, not even Merlin the Wizard, can beat 16 percent."

In order to beat that 16 percent, horseplayers began to look for the "sure thing," some advantage enabling them to become winners, racing's answer to getting money from home without writing. One plunger of the past, "Pittsburgh Phil" Smith, had a philosophy all his own: "A man who has not an opinion of his own and the ability to stick to it in the face of all kinds of arguments has not one chance in a million to beat the races for any length of time." Another plunger of days long gone by, the aptly named "Bet-a-Million" Gates, who made his presence known at tracks for betting anywheres up to $100,000 in one swell foop, believed there was nothing so sure as a sure thing. Gates, who always liked the odds in his favor, was famous for, one time, betting the wealthy John Drake $11,000 on whose piece of bread, drenched in coffee, would attract the most flies. Gates won because he had not bothered to let Drake know he had put six spoonfuls of sugar in his cup before dunking his slice of bread.

Another successful speculator of the past was the infamous Arnold Rothstein, the reputed mastermind behind the 1919 Black Sox World Series fix. Rothstein, known for having his "betting commissioners," or beards, bet anywheres between $20,000 and $30,000 on a single race, all at separate windows so no one would see how much they were plunking down, believed that a man's reach was only limited by his lack of ingenuity and reached out for information, because as he put it, "Information, sound information, is what you need at a racetrack." Rothstein's method of acquiring such information was by doling out various remittances to those who gave it to him. As he confided to one writer, "I go to the leading trainers and say, 'Tell me if your horse is right. If he is, I'll bet one thousand or two thousand dollars for you. But don't double-cross me.' In this way, I get the best information." It was that type of information Rothstein received just before the running of the 1921 Travers Stakes, when he heard that the favorite was experiencing "some problems," enabling him to win $500,000.

One group looking for Rothstein-type information is the "seagulls," so-called for their propensity for scavenging for bits and pieces of information. Looking for feedbox noise with their eyes rather than their ears, they either mill around, stalking those they identify as smart money—be they heavy hitters, trainers, owners, or even $20-a-day grooms—and follow them to the windows, or station themselves near the windows ready to drift into line directly behind them to cash in on their selections. All in the belief that these people, in almost conspiratorial terms called "they," have some inside poop or are on the cusp of pulling off a betting coup.

It is the belief that some information—any information, even of the nefarious kind—would enable those wearied victims of racing's unkindness to strike it rich that perpetuates them. Trying to shake the gods of ill fortune who have dogged their steps, rather than be tortured by visions of what might have been, they dream of the day they will make their fortune by putting a few bob on a sure thing. And, always, they invoke the name of Art Rooney, who, in one of those stories of a little white hue, was rumored to have broken a bookmaker's bank one day at Saratoga, using the grubstake to found the Pittsburgh Steelers. But, as one who was there tells the story, not so much demytholizing it as fleshing it out, "it wasn't at Saratoga, but at the old Empire City track, where he beat the bookmaker, Erickson, for a quarter of a million. It was just before Saratoga opened and Art told them to bring the money on up and he'd settle up and play some more." Never mind the specifics, the story still brings a smile to the unrelieved black scowl on many a face found at the tracks.

Information or no information, in a game ripe for stratagems and spoils, the surest way to the surest thing is the fixing of a race. Down through the long, winding—and sometimes crooked—road of racing, more than a few whose souls were as black as their fingernails have resorted to the artifice of grafting. Sometimes a betting coup is pulled off when something happened to the odds-on favorite and the gamblers knew the favorite was going to run off the board, as was the case when Sysonsby, one of racing's all-time greats, was drugged in the 1904 Futurity, suffering his only loss; or when the 1904 Belmont Stakes winner Delhi ran sluggishly after sponges were inserted far up his nose, blocking his breathing passages.

More frequently, though, the coup happens when a long shot surprisingly comes home a winner. This happens most oft when a horse, called a "ringer," exuding the essential oils of determination, is substituted for another who might have been in a trance for all the interest he had shown in previous races, there being oysters on the half shell with more divine fire.

Back in the early 1900s, a faint whisper in the history of horse racing, there was a horse named Ulf, a big black horse with a white face who won race after race on the St. Louis tracks, his owner and his friends betting heavily on him and cleaning up the betting ring. Ultimately, the bookies became wise to him and put up prohibitive prices, making it all but impossible to make money cashing a bet on Ulf. One day, a horse named High License, by High Ball out of Miss Bourbon, was entered, and the owners of Ulf told their friends to get down on High License, hook, line, and wallet. When the betting opened, the bookies, never having heard of High License, greedily accepted the rush of money on the horse. As the bugler started to blow his "Boots and Saddle" call, there was pandemonium in the betting ring, with every book in the long line loaded down with High License money, so much so that, if the horse won, they would all be relegated to the poorhouse. And so, they told the track officials, one of whom swore he'd seen the horse before, saying, "I'd take my oath he was Ulf, but Ulf has a white face and four white stockings and this horse is black all over." After the race, which High License won by a proverbial city block, the track manager walked into the winner's circle and grabbed hold of the horse's bit. Some of the black paint rubbed off the horse's nose onto his hand and, when the manager patted the horse on the nose, as horsemen will, his hand stuck in the black paint when he drew it away. Pruned of his painted fig leaf, he proved to be a horse of a different color: Ulf. Quietly, he was disqualified and his owners banned from the track.

Jump-skip, dear readers, to the late 1920s and early '30s, when a master painter named Paddy Barrie, who used henna dyes that withstood repeated washings instead of water-soluble dyes that sometimes washed off, ran several ringers who stayed, in the words of one correspondent, "rung." With what might be called a discerning touch with the bottle, Barrie was able to transform dark chestnut geldings into light chestnuts with a white stripe, or anything else you wanted, short of a picture of irises at Arles. Finally, after pulling off numerous coups up and down the Eastern seaboard, the Pinkerton detectives caught up with him.

More recently, in 1978, there was another ringer case, this one at Chicago's Hawthorne Race Track when a long shot named Charollius won the second half of the daily double, worth $113.60. However, Charollius, a horse of indifferent accomplishment who ran as if there were sand in his gears, was, in reality, a much better horse named Roman Decade. The day after the race, Hawthorne burned down in what police called "a fire of suspicious origins."

The fire, it was later determined, had been set by someone with a burning desire to hide any and all evidence of the switch in horses, in this case falsified foal certificates. Those certificates, issued by the Jockey Club had, since 1946, also contained the tattoo marking of the horse, a combination of letters and numbers branded upon the horse's upper lip as a way of identifying every horse by a horse identifier who goes stall to stall before every race to make sure the tattoo so entered on the certificate matches that of the horse entered in the race. An annual report of the time by the Thoroughbred Racing Protective Bureau (the TRPB), a group now under the jurisdiction of the Jockey Club, proudly trumpeted, "We know where the horse was tattooed, on what date, the name of the technician who did the branding, the original Jockey Club certificate number and we can produce a picture of what the tattoo brand looks like."

Still, all of the protective measures put in place did not make ringing obsolete. In 1945, a five-year-old son of the famed War Admiral, who had supposedly been retired when he had been claimed for $3,750, showed up running under the alias of Allpulch, a horse who needed a month's notice to race, winning at Rockingham Park and Narragansett until detected and finally retired for real by the TRPB. And, more recently, in 2002, the U.S.

Attorney for the Southern District of Florida indicted two men for running a horse named Forty Two under the names Almost Impossible and Swing-A-Tune at Calder and Penn National, the scam uncovered when the bogus horses' foal certificates were compared to their lip tattoos.

Such zealous policing for ringers has forced those in the fourth ring of racing's netherworld to look for other ways of fixing races, one of the oldest being the administration of performance-enhancing drugs to the horse. Over the years, several unabashed trainers, facetiously called "chemists" by their colleagues, have worked that voodoo they do so well helping horses, like Sir Barton, who, in the words of one correspondent, "ran with all his lights turned on."

To some, doping is as unthinkable as Santa Claus suffering from vertigo, Captain Bligh from sea sickness, Mary having a little lamb. But its practitioners and some members of the old school see nothing wrong with helping a horse out—that is, unless the trainer of the so-called hot horse fouls up the form players by running his horse hot one day and cold the next time out.

Doping was so prevalent that Red Smith wrote the following ode to hophorses on New Year's Day, 1946:

> Roll the aged ephedrine out;
> Lift your needles high!
> Greet the new year with a shout,
> Here's morphine in your eye!
> Light a reefer for your nag
> And if he wants a snifter
> Don't offer Dobbin Kaffee Hag;
> Caffeine make him swifter.
> Snow—heroin—benezedrine—
> Essence of the poppy—
> Surely there has never been
> A New Year's Day so hoppy!

Despite all the tests developed to uncover cases of doping, from saliva tests to sophisticated lab tests, doping still occurs, many times masked by a concoction known as a "milkshake." Only recently, under the felicious headline, NAGGING QUESTIONS, a *Sports Illustrated* article told of an owner and his trainer who both had previous violations for drugging horses and were, almost like the watering of last year's crops, winning race after race at Gulfstream Park. Believing that all such signs should be strictly observed as railroad crossings, the track officials went to the extreme of taking the sawn-off leg of one of their horses who had dropped dead on the track and shipping it off for a necropsy.

A far more subtle, though more difficult, method of fixing a race is by getting to those jockeys who are condemned to a lifetime of cold cuts, with steak and potatoes off limits, and looking to supplement both their diet and their income. Usually such scams are pulled off at tracks that command less public attention than the international trade balance, where paying Paul to rob Peter is less obvious, because of the class of horses and the class of jockeys, such as the small New England tracks where, a few years back, the Winterhill Mob plied their crooked trade. One gambler who had been caught throwing money in the direction of jocks in New Jersey complained in court that such a practice wouldn't work at New York tracks like Aqueduct and Belmont, "Because those bastards would want too much money. Did you ever see the cars they drive and the women they have?"

Which is not to say that top-flight jockeys would consider riding like eight spots in a jack-high game even if they were offered the money—two jockeys, Ted Atkinson and Conn McCreary, cooperated with Federal authorities several years ago after being approached by gamblers.

But, fix or no, any bettor who has ever pawned more than a few promises backing a horse that lost for reasons as unexplainable as why Hawaii has Interstate highways, believes full well that there must be some taint of a conspiracy, up to and including the presence of a grassy knoll, behind the result. It's their nature.

Beginning in the early A.M., when eager bettors first arrive, there to lean over the rail like Monday morning wash watching the workouts through the rest of the morn as the crowd builds, the track is, by crowd standards, relatively quiet with great consideration and forebearance shown those reading their *Racing Forms*, most exchanging pleasantries and opinions on their pick du jour in muted tones, so as not to be overheard by those gifted in the art of eavesdropping.

As time for the first race draws near, the decibel level begins to build in anticipation of the day's races. Now can be seen lines forming at every betting window, money and betting philosophies at the ready. Over here, you'll see the chalk brigade, those fearless champions of the overdog who bet on the favorite. Over there, those who are betting something that sounds like "four-one for the poor one," an exacta combination which, according to superstition, will break a losing streak, or some other cockamamie system, many of which couldn't stand up to the vaguest sort of examination. And, everywhere, turf speculators buying $200 worth of hope for two minutes at two dollars, never giving their chances a second thought, the first covered 'em all, thank you!

The gates suddenly swung open and, as the horses exploded out of the gate like a spontaneous combustion, the bettors jumped up and down like 6,000 little kids who had just missed the boat to their annual picnic, screaming and urging their horses on, the noise almost drowning out the track announcer whose call sounded to the uninitiated as something like: "One One was one racehorse, Two Two was one too . . . One One won race one, Two Two won one too."

And then, just as quickly, the race was over and, almost as if a choirmaster had waved it off, so too was the noise. In its place could be heard a few as giddy as Captain John Smith after Pocahontas went his bail, while the predominant sound heard from the parishioners was a low hum of voices, desolate, almost keening, moaning something along the order of "I couldn't pick a winner if I waited 'til they crossed the finish line to bet."

Sometimes, between their private weeping and gnashing of teeth, they publicly vent their frustrations in the direction of the horses, with words such as "Put him back with the claimers!" Sometimes they take it out on the jockey, as happened to Eddie Arcaro after the post parade for an upcoming race, when a man called out, "Eddie, Eddie, please look at me, Eddie." Arcaro ignored him at first, but after the man cooed "Eddie, Eddie, please . . ." several more times, turned toward him. Now shaking his fist, the man screamed out, "You stink!" and several other florid libels against his nature, even questioning his parentage.

The process would be repeated again and again, up to eight times a day, the majority reduced to the lowest ebb possible in their fortunes. And yet, before they were reduced to doing their brother-could-you-spare-a-dime routines, they were back at the windows nursing unconquerable hope as they tried to make up arrearages.

As the afternoon wore on, the floor of the track became matted, wall to wall, with discarded tickets, those souvenirs of failure nobody wanted to keep. However, those vestiges of some-body's loss were to be somebody else's gain as "stoopers," bent double like the carpenter's rule, almost as if their tie was caught in their fly, continually studied the floor for tickets that had been thrown away.

One of the most imaginative stoopers was a woman who fre-quented the New York racing circuit tracks called "Rosemary Rosary," since she was always found seated on a bench near the cashier's office, rosary beads in hand. Rosemary combined stoop-ing with being a "percenter," who made her living cashing in big winning tickets for gamblers who had developed an allergy to the IRS. Rosemary operated on the premise that her client had, say, a Trifecta winning ticket that paid $6,000 and, if he cashed it in he would receive $4,380 ($6,000 minus 27 percent, or $1,620), and still be required to list the winnings on his income tax return. For her services, Rosemary would cash the ticket, using her Social Se-curity number, then give her client $4,000 and pocket $380. When it came time to file her income taxes, Rosemary, who had been picking up discarded $100 losing tickets after each race, was cov-ered, the IRS allowing anyone filing to "deduct your losses only to the extent of your winnings."

But, for most, the bettors just pick themselves up, dust them-selves off, and shuffle off in the direction of the parking lot, hop-ing they have better luck in picking their car or bus out from among the thousands in the parking lot than in picking the winner from just eight in a race. And, remembering writer Pete Axthelm's line "It's hard to die at the racetrack, because you're always trying to hang around for the good thing that runs tomorrow," they'll be back tomorrow, because they believe the faint of heart never won so much as a scrap of paper. For the bettors, there is no such thing as no hope, no rent to pay, and no tomorrow.

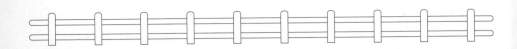

Jockey Edgar Prada and long-shot winner Sarava of the Belmont Stakes, a Visa Triple Crown Event (Copyright © Getty Images, Getty Images North America).

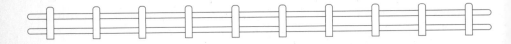

6

THE FUTURE

L
ike the two ad execs meeting and one asking the other, "What's new and improved?" racing today is. Then again, it had to do something to repackage itself after years of just standing there without even asking for a blindfold, cigarette dangling from its lips, as it watched its patrons—a thinning number with thinning hair—go to their final payoff, its place atop the gambling mountain go to casinos, and its hold on the sporting public go to other sports.

How did racing, one of the three major sports in America at the turn of the twentieth century, ever get to the point at which it had become so marginalized that it stood on the cusp of tombstones-and-local-papers-please-carry? It's a long story, one that took an entire century to play out, of a sport whose powers-that-be-and-were sat in racing's counting rooms counting out the money while waiting to hear echoes of an earlier day. For being a major sport is a transitory act, one subject to discontinuation without further notice unless worked at. And racing had hardly worked at it.

Take television, for instance, that magic lantern that, throughout the '50s, transported more people to fantasyland than Aladdin's wish giver ever dreamed of. As this new medium stood poised to train the glare of its cameras on the world of sports, some of the greatest thinkers since the last time Millard Fillmore's cabinet gathered in concert assembled, either through arrogance or short-sightedness, decided that, beyond the Triple Crown, they could do without TV, fearing that such free coverage would eat into their hot-dog and admission revenues. And so, while television was "growing" other sports that made use of it, like golf and football, horse racing lost out on an opportunity to expose its product to an entire generation of future fans.

Taking their cue from racing's cold shoulder, TV execs reciprocated, turning the other. By 1977, when every bowl game, except maybe the Toilet Bowl, was televised, and baseball was a staple second only to soap operas, the networks devoted just five telecasts a year to major racing events. And those averaged just fifty-six minutes per telecast, the least airtime of all so-called major sports. It was so bad that, in 1981, the local Lexington, Kentucky, station—which racing writer Philip Von Borries called "right in the middle of thoroughbred country, the capital of the world"—preempted the televising of the Arlington Million, racing's first million-dollar thoroughbred race, a nail-biter of a race between John Henry and The Bart, for a Cincinnati Reds baseball game.

One of the few races televised was the Kentucky Derby. When Roone Arledge first became head of ABC Sports, he was given a mandate by the then-head of ABC television, Tom Moore, to go out and get events that would make the network the recognized leader in sports around the world. "There were," said Moore, "just so many events and you weren't going to create any more." And so it was, after years of trying, that Arledge managed to land the Derby for ABC in the mid-'70s, ending a reign of twenty-six years for CBS. One of ABC's announcers for their first Derby was Howard Cosell, who spent much of his time boasting to and preening for fellow members of the media, one of whom, caught at the same table with Cosell, hollered across the Churchill Downs media room, "Come over and help me listen to Cosell." But even Cosell could be one-upped, as was the case when he shouted across the media room at columnist Frank Beerman, who had damned with faint praise ABC's coverage of the 1975 Derby when track announcer Chic Anderson called Prince Thou Art the winner instead of Foolish Pleasure. "I know every winner of the first 100 Derbys," screamed Cosell. And Beerman yelled back, "Fine, but I still don't know the winner of this year's!"

And research? Don't ask; they didn't. Not too long ago, horse racing was the only sport that had never undertaken research to discover the demographics of its fans, other than to check out-of-state license plates in its parking lots. What little research they did have showed the average racing fan was somewhere between fifty-two years of age and death.

Then, there were promotions. Or lack thereof. That is, until 1969, when Bill Veeck—who had declared in his autobiography, *Veeck—As in Wreck*, "Look for me under the arc lights, boys, I'll be back"—came back, this time not to the sport with which he was identified, baseball, but to horse racing, as president and part owner of East Boston's rundown racing emporium known as Suffolk Downs, a track built some thirty-four years before on the site of an East Boston dump, and which had reverted pretty much to its original state.

With tacit and tactical understanding of promotions—after all, he had introduced bat days, electronic scoreboards, and even a midget to baseball, all in the name of promotion—Veeck, believing that "anything you do to enhance sales is a promotion," and that "refurbishing is a promotion, of sorts," immediately initiated a $1 million renovation program designed to make Suffolk Downs presentable. Without paying full faith and credit to racing's musty traditions, the colorful Veeck embarked upon a series of promotions, reopening Suffolk Downs with a $10,000 Lady Godiva Handicap featuring the then-controversial jockettes, "Eight fillies on eight fillies," and followed that up with the by-now-recognizable Veeckian gifts to those attending, including two thousand coloring books, a lifetime supply of balloons, and one thousand hot dogs. In more horseplay, minstrels strolled through the grandstand. And, to lure more women to the track, he designed a program to exchange trading stamps for losing tix. It was all vintage Veeck. And it was promotion, something horse racing had never seen.

Perhaps Veeck's greatest promotion was his nonacceptance of an almost universal prohibition of children at the track. Believing that cultivating future fans was the very essence of a sport's future, Veeck went to the Massachusetts Superior Court and won a decision reversing the Massachusetts Racing Commission's ban on children at the track. "I may not know much about horses," Veeck admitted, "but I do know that we've got to get the young ones to come to develop new players." And then, in a takeoff on an old Milton Berle joke—where a youngster tells his mother his father took him to the zoo and "one of the animals paid $30"—added impishly, "Why shouldn't kids be able to see what their old man is up to?"

In 1971, New York racing was blindsided by something called OTB—more formally known as Off-Track Betting. Common wisdom had it that Off-Track Betting was enacted for a moral issue: Its establishment would put the neighborhood bookie out of business. Then again, common wisdom had lost its virginity years before. The real reason the New York State legislature passed the bill creating OTB was to painlessly raise revenues.

But the establishment of Off-Track Betting was painful for New York tracks, almost putting them out of business. Soon, OTB betting parlors were sprouting up like weeds on every New York street corner offering the $2 bettors a chance to lose their money in a more convenient manner than by going off to the track. No longer did the improvers of the breed have to spend a day at the races, paying for transportation, food, and whathaveyou's. Now, for a 6 percent surcharge, they could march into any one of 200 friendly local OTBs, put their money down, and still have enough left over for their copy of the *Daily Racing Form.*

The results were predictable. Whereas the average daily attendance at thoroughbred tracks had declined from 8,706 to 8,215 in the previous decade, it now dropped precipitously, falling 19 percent, with the first Aqueduct meeting showing 5,500 fewer fans per day and an average on-track betting handle down 14 percent, or $500,000 per day.

Like touts watching the tote board, the politicians in Albany began watching OTB's effect on the New York racing industry. It took no giant mental balloon ascension for them to realize they would either have to come to their senses quickly, or that racing in their state would come to its knees almost as quickly. And so, they enacted legislation to combat OTB, including legalizing Sunday racing, lowering the betting age from twenty-one to eighteen, and, finally, giving the New York Racing Association (NYRA) flexibility in ticket pricing.

The New York Racing Association, for its part, tried something they had always considered anathema and beneath them to bring back their patrons: promotions. First, they authorized exotic betting with perfectas, superfectas, quinellas, and all manner of gimmick betting to bring the OTB player back out to the track.

However, each of these innovations was copied by OTB. And sometimes improved upon. The NYRA even advertised the pleasures of attending beautiful Belmont and the less-beautiful Aqueduct. But those who regularly attended OTB parlors were not interested in spending money for track admissions, programs, transportation, and the like, money that could be plowed back into a $2 bet on a sure thing.

Finally, looking for an instant alchemy that could pay dividends, the NYRA accepted the inevitable, and reluctantly resorted to promotions, pure and simple, in an effort to attract young people and families to its tracks, the first of which was something called Bonus Week, a promotion-a-day carnival in the fall of '77, marketed under the umbrella theme "Don't Miss the Most Exciting Week in the History of Belmont." Bonus Week started off with Tip Day, with everyone in attendance being given free felt-tip pens, a book titled *The ABCs of Thoroughbred Racing*, and an opportunity to hear oddsmaker Jimmy the Greek demonstrate why he was not in a class with the fabled gambler Nick the Greek. The next day was something called Big Apple Food Festival Day, with courses of ethnic foods served up to those in attendance by a cross-section of New York restaurants. The third day was Priceless Day, a day when free admission was granted to the grandstand. Then came a day when everyone could have their pictures taken with the jockey of his or her choice, and a chance to purchase a pair of binoculars at wholesale prices. And on Friday, the fifth day of Bonus Week, came Doubles Day, a euphemistic handle for a promotion that has been known for years in the advertising trade as "twofers," with two tix to the grandstand available for the price of one. And the week was capped off on Saturday with Glen Campbell Day, with the Wichita Lineman singing for the benefit of those players who had enough left over after Bonus Week to still lay it on the morning line.

However, it was next to impossible to turn around years of erosion and, worse, inattentiveness, with a one-week effort.

The NYRA's former constituency, the bettor, weaned away by OTB, was not about to return to the track just because of Glen Campbell, Jimmy the Greek, and twofers.

Still racing, long an odds-on favorite to continue its holding pattern, paid no-nevermind to signals that should have been as observed as railroad crossings, such as declining attendance, the graying of its fans, and the redirection of the gambling dollar, once theirs but now going to casinos, instead of viewing all such great truths as blasphemous.

For hadn't the '70s produced some of the greatest legends ever known to racingkind, horses like Secretariat, Affirmed, Alydar, Seattle Slew, Bold Forbes, Spectacular Bid, and Forego, horses that could take their place in the starting gate and make any dues-paying fan feel good? And the '80s saw new money drive prices for bloodstock to such stratospheric levels that it was a wonder they didn't come with farms? And the '90s introduced a new series, the superrich Dubai World Cup Series, giving owners a chance to pick up another mil or two?

Despite this, the one event that served as a hinge for racing's comeback was the introduction of one of the most imaginative ideas to come down racing's pike since man first determined to sit astride a horse and race him. And it gave nourishment to those in the establishment that thought their sport was anything but a sport suffering a severe case of Indian summer. But, like the lion thought to be dead just because no one had heard it roar lately, it was still full of vitality: the Breeders' Cup.

The Breeders' Cup was the creation of John R. Gaines, one of the leading commercial breeders in the United States, and backed

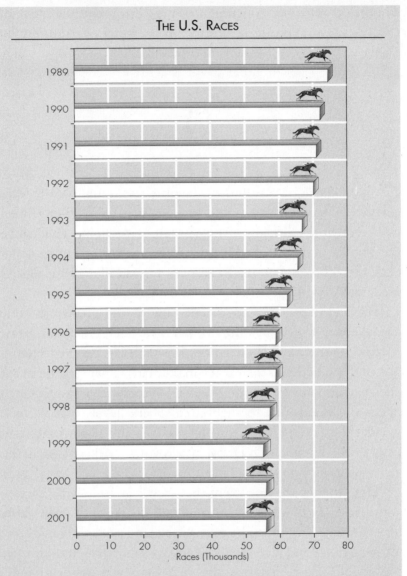

THE U.S. RACES

A year after its first increase since 1989, the number of thoroughbred races run in the United States in 2001 declined 0.6 percent. To a large extent, the decline was accounted for by meet cancellations at Playfair Racecourse and Salem/Lone Oak Park, which together ran 54 days in 2000. Curtailed racing at several small- to mid-size tracks also contributed to the decrease.

wholeheartedly by his brothers-in-breeding, concerned that the price of bloodstock and stud fees was inextricably tied to the size of purses. In order to keep prices at their record levels, Gaines proposed a $13 million day at the races, with seven races featuring the world's best horses. And so was born the Breeders' Cup, a season-ending day that redefined the racing calendar, giving racing not only a perfect bookend to the start of the season with the Derby, but also a final punctuation point to match football's Super Bowl and baseball's World Series. However, unlike the World Series, which, in the words of one wag, "was hardly for the world championship, but merely for the championship of the northeastern quadrant of the Western Hemisphere," the eight races of the Breeders' Cup were for world supremacy—as was proven time and again with horses from France and England and Ireland and all points north, east, west, and south winning.

The Breeders' Cup has become the most prominent group of races in the sport, with owners and trainers, from early summer on, pointing their horses toward it as the ultimate in racing. In fact, from 1984 through 2000, 122 of 153 winners of the prestigious Eclipse Award (excluding steeplechasers) have run in Breeders' Cup races. And on nine occasions, the Breeders' Cup Classic winner was named divisional champion, with eight of them— Ferdinand (1987), Sunday Silence (1989), Black Tie Affair (1991), A. P. Indy (1992), Cigar (1995), Skip Away (1997), and Tiznow (2000)—further honored as Horse of the Year.

The first edition of the Breeders' Cup, to mix a metaphor, kicked off at Hollywood Park on November 10, 1984, when a crowd of 64,254 watched Chief's Crown win the first race, the $1 million Juvenile, and, six races later, supplementary entry Wild Again edge Gate Dancer and Slew o' Gold for the largest purse in racing history, $4 mil. After its successful debut, the Breeders' Cup, harboring migratory ambitions, went, in a moveable feast, like the NFL's Super Bowl, to a different track each year, making headlines and fans in some of the most memorable races in recent racing history: Personal Ensign in a head-to-head battle with Winning Colors in the '88 Distaff, again at Hollywood; Fraise upsetting Sky Classic, the favorite, by a nose in the '92 Turf at Gulfstream Park; and, to quote announcer John Durkin, "The incomparable, invincible Cigar" laying waste to the landscape, roaring past L'Carrier in the '95 Classic at Belmont. The Classic also added two of the sport's greatest moments to its already growing list of such stirring snapshots: the stretch duel between Ferdinand and Alysheba at Hollywood Park in 1987, with Bill Shoemaker urging Ferdinand home by a nose, and, the following year, with Alysheba emerging from the deep shadows at Churchill Downs to win by a half-length over Seeking the Gold.

As the popularity of the Breeders' Cup grew—as did the Cup itself, adding an eighth race in 1999, the Filly and Mare Turf—so, too, did the amount of ink given the event, as writers reduced their pencils down to stubs covering the Cup as if it were the Creation of the World, Part II, with stories, sidebars, and features, including quotes, from everyone associated with the Breeders' Cup—up to the horses' whinnies. All of a sudden, all was right in racing's heavens, or so it seemed, the sport, like Dolly, back where it belonged, on the front sports page (as opposed to where it previously had been under) the shipping news.

The success of the Breeders' Cup led the Old Guard to reassess their traditional approach to the sport; to wonder if their confidence in Gibraltar wasn't misplaced as they watched their portion of the gambling dollar shrink to just 9 percent of the total in the face of competition, mostly from newly minted casinos;

and that if waiting for the old days to return wasn't somehow akin to some hypothesis or other about a watched pot.

And, so, as the scales fell from the eyes and they suddenly realized they either had to reinvent the racing wheel or face becoming obsolete, just as they had seventy years before, when they adopted new technology in using pari-mutuel machines to counteract the wave of antigambling legislation, they now adopted new technology to counteract the erosion of their market.

To tap into the gambling mania that swept the country in the late '80s and early '90s—not incidentally, a mania that also swept away their customers—tracks began to offer their patrons simulcasting, full-card telecasting from other tracks. Witnessing the success of simulcasting, tracks then introduced off-track betting via telephone and computer and, in those states where favorable legislation allowed them, slot machines, all in the name of "up your profits" by upping their patrons' opportunities to bet.

However, such innovations always come with a price to pay and ribbons to be untied. Some, notably track owners like Lonny Powell, then the head of Santa Anita, was quoted as saying, "The world of simulcast and off-track betting has been an outstanding source of purses. At the end of the day, it's not how the bucket is filled, as long as the handle grows, that's how the industry will develop." Others, with a far more jaundiced view, questioned whether racing was, like Paul with the proceeds of the gold brick road, going off in a new direction. A direction that they were totally unfamiliar or uncomfortable with, where, unlike bingo in a church, winners did not have to be present.

Many critics, examining the contents of the bottle, not just the bottle itself, were confused by the entry of the new players racing had attracted. For these were a totally different race of people from the old-line handicappers, younger high-techie figure dancers with the attention span of a ferret on a double espresso, who didn't have the patience to wait twenty-five minutes between races nor go

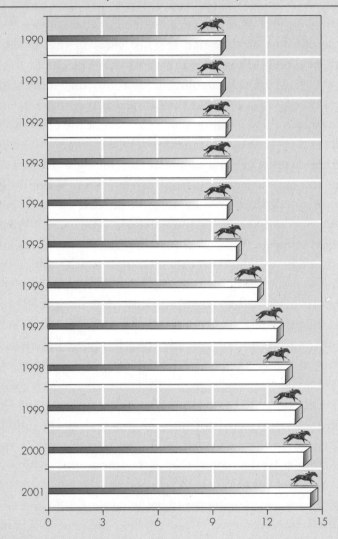

U.S. Pari-Mutuel Handle, 1990–2001
(in Millions of Dollars)

Pari-mutuel handle wagered on thoroughbred racing in the United States during 2001 (including separate pools first reported in 2000) increased 1.6 percent, while total North American handle advanced 1.7 percent. Gains continued to come exclusively from the off-track sector, which accounted for 85.5 percent of U.S. handle. *Source:* Copyright © The Jockey Club. All rights reserved.

through the painful process of handicapping. They were less horse fanciers than pure gamblers, the types William Faulkner described in his essay "Kentucky: Saturday: May" as those "who don't like horses—the ones who would not touch a horse or go near it, who never mounted one nor ever intend to; who can and do risk and lose their shirts on a horse they have never seen."

This new breed of bettor was behind the recent attempt to manipulate an Ultra Pick Six ticket on the 2002 Breeders' Cup at Arlington Park. The plan, a simple one, as all great swindles tend to be, was a variation on the old post-posting scam, except, this time, it was done by computers. One of the trio of bettors-cum-swindlers placed his Pick Six bets via touch-tone dialing through Catskill Off-Track Betting Corp. of Pomona, New York, using a week-old account to place $1,152 worth of wagers while a confederate at the Delaware offices of Autotote, which processed the bets for Catskill, used his password to enter the Catskill computers and change the bets on the first four races before the computers forwarded them to Arlington Park's hub. They then bet all the horses running in the final two races to assure a winning Pick Six ticket. Were it not for the fact that Volpone, a 40-to-1 shot, won the last race, the Classic, making theirs the only winning ticket, their scam might have gone undetected.

Regardless of whether the money came from racing or gambling fans, it came. In buckets. Enough to enable tracks to refurbish their facilities, add to their purse structure, and encourage multiple-track ownership by corporations who suddenly saw the profits to be made in the once-dormant sport of racing.

And more than enough to underwrite an organization, the National Thoroughbred Racing Association (NTRA), which would coordinate the marketing efforts of the entire sport, one heretofore given to an internicine push-me–pull-you struggle between its various factions. The NTRA's duties included everything from advertising to sponsorships, to television to research and just about every other component of the marketing umbrella, all of which had been sorely overlooked before.

With everything now seemingly in place, racing is poised to regain its proper position as one of the premier sports in America, a position it held at the turn of the previous century. It is in the belief that this goal was more than attainable that NTRA Commissioner Tim Smith optimistically cited positive developments in the sport, stating that 2001 was a year of "record parimutuel handle and purses for the eighth year in a row, another year of growth in fan interest in our sport, and (of) impressive momentum for our sport's signature events, the Visa Triple Crown and the Breeders' Cup."

The Fates have always been uncommonly partial to comebacks, and racing is staging one now, one worthy of a Forego—or, for those old enough to remember, Silky Sullivan. And given lie to the slander time had passed it by. There's life in the old gal yet. Full of enough breath to becloud a mirror.

APPENDIX

CHAPTER 1—THE TRACKS

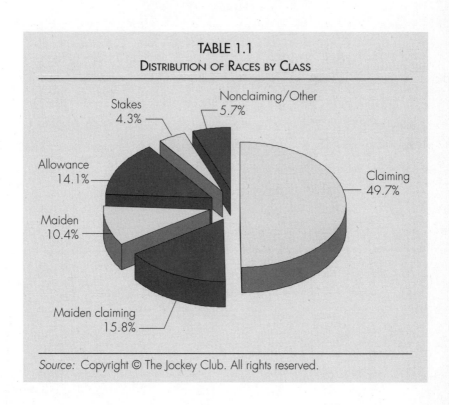

TABLE 1.1
DISTRIBUTION OF RACES BY CLASS

Stakes 4.3%

Nonclaiming/Other 5.7%

Allowance 14.1%

Claiming 49.7%

Maiden 10.4%

Maiden claiming 15.8%

TABLE 1.2
Handicap Weight Allowances

Distance	Age	Weight
One-half mile	3	123
	4	130
	5 or older	130
Six furlongs	3	121
	4	130
	5 or older	130
One mile	3	115
	4	126
	5 or older	126
One mile and ¼	3	113
	4	126
	5 or older	126
One mile and ½	3	111
	4	126
	5 or older	126
Two miles	3	109
	4	126
	5 or older	126

TABLE 1.3
DISTRIBUTION OF ALL NORTH AMERICAN RACES BY PURSE FOR 2001

Range of Purses ($)	No. of Races	Total Purse ($)
499 or less	0	0
500–999	19	15,623
1,000–1,999	659	1,059,565
2,000–2,999	1,089	2,610,864
3,000–3,999	1,981	6,631,876
4,000–4,999	3,741	17,090,891
5,000–5,999	4,995	26,797,792
6,000–6,999	3,357	21,602,071
7,000–7,999	4,476	33,100,248
8,000–8,999	3,011	25,123,906
9,000–9,999	3,338	31,271,720
10,000–12,499	6,443	70,891,506
12,500–14,999	4,747	64,062,965
15,000–19,999	6,019	103,216,507
20,000–24,999	3,686	81,568,015
25,000–29,999	3,092	83,163,912
30,000–39,999	3,665	124,409,883
40,000–49,999	3,033	132,746,671
50,000–74,999	2,029	114,030,094
75,000–99,999	303	24,336,119
100,000–199,999	585	71,946,407
200,000–299,999	145	32,954,952

(continued)

TABLE 1.3   (Continued)

Range of Purses ($)	No. of Races	Total Purse ($)
300,000–399,999	30	9,602,975
400,000–499,999	19	7,980,575
500,000–749,999	42	22,069,750
750,000–999,999	15	11,829,000
1,000,000 and up	19	26,223,480
Totals	60,538	1,146,337,367

TABLE 1.4
THOROUGHBRED PURSE
DISTRIBUTION STRUCTURE

Finish	Average (%)	Belmont (%)	Santa Anita (%)	Churchill Downs (%)	Suffolk Downs (%)
1	59.7	60	55	65	60
2	20.1	22	20	20	20
3	11.5	12	15	10	10
4	5.9	6	7.5	5	5
5	2.1	None	2.4	None	3
6	.8	None	None	None	2

TABLE 1.5
Oldest Thoroughbred Races

Year	Name
1831	Phoenix Handicap
1860	Queen's Plate Stakes
1864	Travers Stakes
1866	Jerome Handicap
1867	Belmont Stakes Champagne Stakes
1868	Ladies Handicap
1870	Dixie Handicap
1871	Monmouth Oaks
1872	Alabama Stakes
1872	California Derby Preakness Stakes
1874	Juvenile Stakes Withers Stakes
1875	Clarke Handicap Kentucky Derby Kentucky Oaks
1881	Spinaway Stakes

TABLE 1.6
Great Match Races
OF THE
Twentieth Century

Year/Racetrack	Horses	Winner
1920 Kenilworth Park	Man o' War vs. Sir Barton	Man o' War
1923 Belmont Park	Zev vs. Papyrus	Zev
1938 Pimlico Race Course	War Admiral vs. Seabiscuit	Seabiscuit
1942 Narragansett Park	Alsab vs. Whirlaway	Alsab
1947 Belmont Park	Armed vs. Assault	Armed
1955 Washington Park	Swaps vs. Nashua	Nashua
1972 Hollywood Park	Convenience vs. Typecast	Convenience
1974 Hollywood Park	Chris Evert vs. Miss Musket	Chris Evert
1975 Belmont Park	Ruffian vs. Foolish Pleasure	Foolish Pleasure

TABLE 1.7
GREAT HIGHWEIGHTS
HANDICAP CHAMPIONS

Name	Earnings ($)	Era	Top-Weight
Hamburg	60,380	1897–98	135
Whisk Broom II	37,931	1909–13	139
Pan Zareta	39,082	1912–17	140
Exterminator	252,996	1917–24	135
Man O' War	249,465	1919–20	138
Grey Lag	136,715	1920–31	135
Princess Doreen [f]	174,745	1923–27	133
Discovery	195,287	1933–36	139
Devil Diver	261,064	1941–45	136
Stymie	918,485	1943–49	134
Bold Ruler	764,204	1956–58	134
Tom Fool	570,165	1951–53	136
Round Table	1,749,869	1956–59	136
Gun Bow	798,722	1963–65	130
Dr. Fager	1,002,642	1966–68	139
Gamely [f]	574,961	1967–69	131
Forego	1,938,957	1973–78	137
Seattle Slew	1,208,726	1976–78	134

CHAPTER 2—THE OWNERS

TABLE 2.1
THE KENTUCKY DERBY'S
LEADING WINNING OWNERS

Owners	Starts	Wins
Calumet Farm	20	8
Col. E. R. Bradley	28	4
Belair Stud	8	3
W. Condren/J. Cornacchia	2	2
Darby Dan Farm	7	2
Greentree Stable	19	2
Mrs. John D. Hertz	3	2
King Ranch	5	2
George Long	11	2
Meadow Stable	3	2
Harry Payne Whitney	19	2

TABLE 2.2
MAJOR AUCTION SALES
(BY SEASON)

Month	Location	Type
January		
February	Maryland-Timonium	Winter mixed sale
	Kentucky-Keeneland	Winter mixed sale
	Florida-Calder	Two-year-olds in training
March	Texas-Lone Star	Two-year-olds in training
April		
May	Maryland-Timonium	Two-year-olds in training
June		
July	Kentucky-Keeneland	Two-year-olds in training & horses of racing age
August	New York-Saratoga	Yearlings, Stallions
	Texas-Lone Star	Yearlings
September	Canada-Woodbine	Yearlings
	Maryland-Timonium	Yearlings
October	Kentucky-Keeneland	Yearlings
	New York-Belmont	Horses of all ages
November	Kentucky-Keeneland	Fall mixed
December	Maryland-Timonium	Fall mixed
	Texas-Lone Star	Fall mixed
	Kentucky-Keeneland	Fall mixed

TABLE 2.3
RACING CALENDAR

Month	North (Maine to New York)	East (New Jersey to Maryland)	South (Virginia to Florida)	West (Washington to New Mexico)	Other
January Three-year-old starts	Aqueduct	Laurel	Gulfstream Turfway Fair Grounds	Santa Anita	Eclipse Awards
February	Aqueduct	Laurel	Gulfstream Turfway Fair Grounds	Santa Anita	Whirlaway Miracle Wood Fountain of Youth
March	Aqueduct	Laurel	Gulfstream Turfway Fair Grounds	Santa Anita	Louisiana Derby Florida Derby Gotham Tampa Bay Derby San Filipe Stakes UAE Derby Dubia World Cup

Month	Aqueduct	Pimlico	Turfway/Keeneland	Hollywood Park	Stakes
April			Turfway Keeneland	Hollywood Park	Illinois Derby Santa Anita Derby Arkansas Derby Wood Memorial Blue Grass Lexington
May Two-year-olds start running	Belmont	Pimlico	Churchill	Hollywood Park	Oaks Derby Black-eyed Susan Preakness
June	Belmont	Pimlico/Laurel	Calder	Hollywood Park	Belmont
July	Saratoga	Laurel	Calder Ellis Park	Del Mar	Hall of Fame Stakes
August Handicap season starts	Saratoga	Laurel	Florida Calder Ellis Park	Del Mar	Whitney Travers Pacific Classic
September	Belmont Fall H'Cap Championships		Calder Ellis Park Kentucky Downs	Del Mar	

(continued)

TABLE 2.3 (Continued)

Month	North (Maine to New York)	East (New Jersey to Maryland)	South (Virginia to Florida)	West (Washington to New Mexico)	Other
October	Belmont	Laurel	Calder Keeneland	Hollywood Park	
November Northern trainers head South	Aqueduct	Laurel	Calder Turf Way Fair Grounds	Hollywood Park	Breeders' Cup
December	Aqueduct	Laurel	Calder Turf Way Fair Grounds	Santa Anita	Sovereign Awards

TABLE 2.4
TRIPLE CROWN CHAMPIONS

Year	Horse	Owner	Trainer	Jockey
1919	Sir Barton	J. K. L. Ross	H. Guy Bardwell	Johnny Loftus
1930	Gallant Fox	Belair Stud	J. E. Fitsimmons	Earl Sande
1935	Omaha	Belair Stud	J. E. Fitzsimmons	Willie Saunders
1937	War Admiral	Samuel Riddle	George Conway	Charley Kurtsinger
1941	Whirlaway	Calumet Farm	Ben A. Jones	Eddie Arcaro
1943	Count Fleet	Mrs. J. D. Hertz	Don Cameron	Johnny Longden
1946	Assault	King Ranch	Max Hirsch	Warren Mehrtens
1948	Citation	Calumet Farm	Ben A. Jones	Eddie Arcaro
1973	Secretariat	Meadow Stable	Lucien Laurin	Ron Turcotte
1977	Seattle Slew	Karen Taylor	Billy Turner	Jean Cruget
1978	Affirmed	Harbor View Farm	Laz Barrera	Steve Cauthen

TABLE 2.5
BOLD RULER'S
LEGACY
(1954–1971)

Horse	Awards
Secretariat	Horse of the Year Triple Crown winner
Gamely	Champion 3-year-old filly Champion handicap mare twice
Wajima	Champion 3-year-old
Successor	Champion 2-year-old
Bold Lad	Champion 2-year-old
Bold Forbes	Champion 3-year-old
Bold Bidder	Champion handicap horse
Vitriolic	Champion 2-year-old
Queen Empress	Champion 2-year-old filly
Bold Lad (Ireland)	
Lamb Chop	
Queen of the Stage	
What A Pleasure	

Note: Bold Ruler led the American Sire's List eight times. Seven of the ten Kentucky Derby winners of the 1970s can be traced directly to Bold Ruler, with an additional four in the 80s.

CHAPTER 3—THE TRAINERS

TABLE 3.1
KENTUCKY DERBY
LEADING TRAINERS

Trainers	Starts	Wins
Ben A. Jones	11	6
H. J. "Dick" Thompson	24	4
Sunny Jim Fitzsimmons	11	3
* D. Wayne Lukas	36	4
Max Hirsch	14	3
Woodford C. Stephens	14	2
* LeRoy Jolley	13	2
James Rowe Sr.	18	2
H. A. Jimmy Jones	4	2
Lucien Laurin	5	2
Horatio Luro	4	2
Lazaro Barrera	5	2
Henry Forest	2	2
Charlie Whittingham	7	2
* Nick P. Zito	6	2
* Bob Baffert	5	2
* Neil Drysdale	1	1

* Active.

TABLE 3.2
TRAINERS EARNING IN EXCESS OF
$10,000,00 IN PURSES

1. Bob Baffert

2. Bobby Frankel

3. D. Wayne Lukas

TABLE 3.3
ESTIMATED
TRAINING EXPENSES
(QUARTERLY)

Training	$ 80 per day	$7,200 per quarter
Stable supplies	300 per month	900 per quarter
Veterinarian	400 per month	1,200 per quarter
Blacksmith	100 per month	300 per quarter
Transportation	200 per month	600 per quarter
Administrative	600 per month	1,800 per quarter
	Total:	$12,000 per quarter

TABLE 3.4
GREAT GELDINGS

Name	Earnings ($)	Era
Parole	82,111	1875–84
Roamer	98,828	1913–19
Old Rosebud	74,729	1913–22
Exterminator	252,996	1917–24
Armed	817,475	1944–50
Elkridge	230,680	1941–51
Kelso	1,977,896	1959–66
Bon Nouvel	176,148	1963–68
Fort Marcy	1,109,791	1966–71
Forego	1,938,957	1973–78
John Henry	6,591,860	1977–84

TABLE 3.5
GREAT FILLIES

Name	Earnings ($)	Era
Miss Woodford	118,270	1882–86
Firenze	112,471	1886–91
Beldame	102,135	1903–05
Maskette	77,090	1908–10
Black Helen	61,800	1934–35
Busher	334,035	1944–47
Gallorette	445,535	1944–48
Dark Mirage	362,789	1967–69
Cicada	783,674	1961–64
Ruffian	313,429	1974–75
Chris Evert	679,475	1973–75
Dahlia	1,535,443	1972–76
Riva Ridge	1,111,347	1971–73
Desert Vixen	421,538	1972–75
Dabova Dale	641,621	1978–80
Genuine Risk	646,587	1979–81
Bold 'n Determined	949,599	1979–81
Princess Rooney	1,343,339	1982–84
Lady's Secret	3,021,325	1984–87
Personal Ensign	1,679,880	1986–88
Winning Colors	1,526,837	1987–89
Paseana	3,171,203	1990–95
Go For Wand	1,373,338	1989–90

Note: The 1970s were not only the greatest era of racing fillies but also of women owners.

TABLE 3.6
GREAT AMERICAN
TURF CHAMPIONS

Name	Era
Twenty Grand	1930–35
Round Table	1950s
Fort. Marcy	1966–71
Crystal Water	1970s
Toonerville	1970s
Double Discount	1970s
John Henry	1980

CHAPTER 4—THE JOCKEYS

TABLE 4.1
KENTUCKY DERBY
LEADING WINNING JOCKEYS

Jockeys	Starts	Wins
Eddie Arcaro	21	5
Bill Hartack	12	5
Bill Shoemaker	26	4
Angel Cordero Jr.	17	3
Isaac Murphy	11	3
Earl Sande	8	3
* Gary Stevens	12	3
* Jerry Bailey	9	2
* Eddie Delahoussaye	10	2
Albert Johnson	7	2
Charles Kurtsinger	4	2
Johnny Loftus	6	2
Linus McAtee	7	2
Chris McCarron	14	2
Conn McCreary	10	2
Willie Simms	2	2
* Gary Stevens	11	2
Ron Turcotte	5	2
Ismael Valenzuela	8	2
Jacinto Vasquez	9	2
Jimmy Winkfield	4	2
* Kent Desormeaux	8	2
Chris Antley	8	2

* Active.

TABLE 4.2
JOCKEYS WHO HAVE EARNED
IN EXCESS OF $10,000,000
(ANNUALLY)

1. Jerry Bailey

2. Angel Cordero Jr.

3. Pat Day

4. Kent Desormeaux

5. Chris McCarron

6. Corey Natakani

7. Lafitt Pincay Jr.

8. Mike South

9. Jose Santos

10. Steve Sellers

11. Alex Solix

12. Gary Stevens

TABLE 4.3
LATINO JOCKEYS
KENTUCKY DERBY WINS

Name	Horse	Year
Gustavo Avila	Canonero II	1971
Braulio Baeza	Chateaugay	1963
Jorge Chavez	Monarchos	2001
Angel Cordero Jr.	Canonade	1974
	Bold Forbes	1976
	Spend a Buck	1985
Henry Morero	Dark Star	1953
Lafitt Pincay Jr.	Swale	1984
Ismael Valenzuela	Tim Tam	1953
	Foreward Pass	1968
Patrick Valenzuela	Sunday Silence	1989
Jacinto Vazquez	Foolish Pleasure	1975
	Genuine Risk	1980
Jorge Valasquez	Pleasant Colony	1981

CHAPTER 6—THE FUTURE

TABLE 6.1
LEADING SIMULCASTERS

Name	Tracks
Churchill Downs	Churchill Downs
	Arlington Park
	Calder Race Course
	Ellis Park
	Hollywood Park
	Hoosier Park
Magna Entertainment Corporation	Santa Anita
	Gulfstream Park
	Pimlico Race Course
	Laurel Park
	Lone Star Park at Grand Prairie
	Golden Gate Fields
	Bay Meadows
	Thistledown
	Remington Park
	Portland Meadows
	Great Lakes Downs

TABLE 6.2
BREEDERS' CUP
LEADING OWNERS

	Wins		Earnings ($)
Allen E. Paulson	6	Allen E. Paulson	7,570,000
Eugene V. Klein	4	Frank H. Stronach	4,898,000
Frank H. Stronach	3	Godolphin Racing	4,700,600
Godolphin Racing	3	Overbrook Farm/ W. T. Young	4,387,000
Overbrook Farm/ W. T. Young	3	Daniel Wildenstein	3,917,000
Ogden Phipps	3	Sheikh Mohammed/ Darley Stud	3,730,960
Flaxman Holdings Ltd./ S. Niarchos	3	Ogden Phipps	3,611,000
Daniel Wildenstein	2	Thoroughbred Corp./ Universal Stables	3,257,000
Sheikh Mohammed/ Darley Stud	2	Juddmonte Farms	3,013,200
Thoroughbred Corp./ Universal Stables	2	Sam-Son Farms	2,878,000
Sam-Son Farms	2	Frances A. Genter	2,835,000

TABLE 6.3
Breeders' Cup
Leading Trainers

	Wins		Earnings ($)
Wayne Lukas	16	D. Wayne Lukas	18,015,600
Shug McGaughey III	7	William I. Mott	8,492,560
Neil Drysdale	6	Shug McGaughey III	6,733,560
William I. Mott	5	Andre Fabre	6,435,400
Ron McAnally	4	Neil Drysdale	5,795,840
Andre Fabre	3	Jay Robbins	4,938,400
Patrick Byrne	3	Bobby Frankel	4,311,800
Jay Robbins	2	Charlie Whittingham	4,298,000
Charlie Whittingham	2	Saeed bin Suroor	3,796,200
Saeed bin Suroor	2	Bob Baffert	3,771,480
Bob Baffert	2	Patrick Burne	3,718,000

TABLE 6.4
BREEDERS' CUP
LEADING JOCKEYS

	Wins	Earnings ($)
Pat Day	12	21,718,200
Jerry Bailey	13	14,899,400
Chris McCarron	9	17,669,600
Gary Stevens	8	13,361,160
Mike Smith	8	8,194,200
Eddie Delahoussaye	7	7,775,000
Laffit Pincay Jr.	7	6,811,000
Jose Santos	6	5,828,000
Pat Valenzuela	6	4,202,000
Corey Nakatani	5	6,440,360

GLOSSARY

◡ A ◡

across the board   Bet on a horse to **win, place,** and **show.** If the horse wins, the player collects three ways; if second, two ways; and, if third, one way, losing the win and place bets.

added   When a track adds money in order to reach the established purse value.

agent   Person authorized to act on the behalf of a jockey or owner. A jockey's agent lines up rides for him or her.

all out   Refers to a horse trying to the best of its ability.

allowance race   Race in which the racing secretary determines the weights and eligibility, with allowances made for certain horses.

also-eligible   Horse entered in the race but that cannot start unless another horse is **scratched.**

also-ran   Horse that finishes out of the money.

American Association of Equine Practitioners (AAEPO)   Organization whose role is to improve the health and welfare of the horse.

American Horse Council (AHC)   Lobbying arm of racing.

American Racing Manual   First published complete list of all breeders in America.

American Racing Record   Second newspaper dedicated to thoroughbred racing; it ceased publication in 1930.

American standard   Usually used to refer to an American racing record at a given distance.

American Stud Book   Directory that lists the thoroughbred bloodlines of each registered horse.

anhidrosis   Condition that makes a horse unable to sweat.

apprentice rider   Designation given to a young or newly licensed jockey. The jockey receives a 10-pound weight allowance, except in stakes and handicap races, until achieving five victories. From the fifth victory until the thirtieth victory, the jockey receives a seven-pound allowance. In every race after the thirtieth win, within one year from the fifth win, the apprentice receives a five-pound allowance. In addition, if the apprentice has a signed contract with a given stable, the jockey receives a three-pound allowance for an additional year when riding a horse for that stable.

ascarids   Internal parasites. Also called *roundworms.*

Association of Racing Commissioners International, Inc. (RCI) Organization responsible for reciprocity and rule enforcement.

asterisk   Until 1976, indicated that the horse was of foreign birth. Subsequently, it was replaced by an abbreviation designating the country of origin. It is also used to indicate a riding weight allowance given to a jockey when it is placed behind his name in the daily racing program.

at grass   Refers to horses that have been turned out into the paddock or field.

at the break   Usually refers to the start of a race, up to the first quarter of a mile.

automatic hot walker   Machine used to walk horses in a circle in order to cool them off.

azortaria   Condition in which the muscles of the loins and hind limbs cramp.

ʊ B ʊ

baby race   Race for two-year-olds.

back at the knee   Conformation fault in which the horse's lower leg curves back from the knee to fetlock, which can cause weakness and a poor stride.

back breeding   In breeding, the consistent use of a specific stallion to preserve a desired trait.

backstretch   Personnel who work in the stable area. On the track, it is used to describe the area located across from the grandstand.

bald-faced   Describes a horse with a predominately white face.

bandy-legged   Condition in which a horse's hocks turn outward.

barn sour   Refers to a horse that objects to being ridden away from the barn.

barrel   Area on a horse's body between the forelegs and the loins.

bars   Fleshy area of a horse's mouth, between the front and back teeth, where the **bit** rests.

bat   Jockey's crop or **whip.**

bay   Coat color, usually of a range from light brown to almost black when accompanied by both a black mane and tail; also refers to a horse of this color.

bearing in   Action of a horse not running in a straight line.

behind the bit   Refers to a horse holding its head behind the vertical, thereby decreasing the rider's control. Also called **overbent.**

bends   Type of horseshoe worn for better traction on soft tracks.

Beyers rating   Speed rating affixed to each horse in a race; created by Andrew Beyer.

billet straps   Straps that attach the girth to the saddle.

bit   Part of a bridle that fits in the animal's mouth. It is used to control movements.

blanket finish   When horses finish so close to each other at the wire that a single blanket could cover them.

blaze   Elongated white marking found down the front of a horse's face. Also called a **stripe.**

bleeder   Horse that suffers pulmonary bleeding before or after a race or workout.

blemish   Permanent mark or scar caused by either an injury or disease. **Curbs** and girth galls are blemishes.

blinkers   Small panels worn on the **bridle** to restrict a horse's peripheral vision in order to help the horse maintain focus and avoid distraction.

blistering   Application of a caustic agent, or blister, to the horse's leg; still used in the treatment of a number of conditions, including spavin, ringbone, and **bowed tendon.**

blood horse   Thoroughbred or Arabian horse.

bloodstock   Thoroughbred horses.

blowout   Short, fast workout, usually a day or two before a race, designed to sharpen a horse's speed.

board   Tote board on which odds, betting pools, and other race information is displayed.

boarding stable   Equestrian facility at which an owner may house a horse for a monthly fee.

bobble   Bad step away from the starting gate, sometimes caused by the ground breaking away from under a horse, causing him to duck his head or go to his knees.

bolt   Sudden veer from a straight course.

bone   Measurement around the leg, just below the knee or **hock;** determines the horse's ability to carry weight.

booting   Action of a jockey urging on a horse, derived from riders urging on horses with their feet.

bowed tendon   Rupture of the sheath enclosing the tendon from the knee to the **fetlock joint.**

bow hocks   Where the horse's hocks turn outward; the opposite of **cow hocks.**

boxy hooves   Condition in which a horse has narrow and upright hooves with a small **frog** and closed heel. Also known as club foot.

breakage   Those pennies left over after **pari-mutuel** payoffs are rounded off to the nearest nickel or dime. Breakage is generally split between the track and state and, in some cases, breeding or other funds, in varying proportions.

breakdown   Injury; commonly used to refer to a catastrophic or fatal breakdown.

breaking a maiden   Horse winning its first race.

breeding season   Most commercial breeders want foals to be born shortly after the beginning of the year; thus, to provide a modest cushion against a late-December foal, the breeding season does not begin before Valentine's Day, February 14.

breezing   Working a horse at a moderate speed; less effort than **handily.**

bridle   Equipment on the horse's head that enables the rider to communicate commands. The **bit** and the reins are parts of the bridle.

broken-in; broken to ride   Refers to a horse that has become accustomed to both the rider and the **tack,** at which point the horse can begin training. Also called *greenbroke.*

broken winded   Refers to a horse that has an abnormal breathing pattern due to chronic obstructive pulmonary disease (COPD), also known as *heaves.*

brood mare   Female horse used for breeding purposes.

brushing   When the hoof or shoe hits the inside of the opposite leg; caused by poor conformation or action.

brushing boots   Equipment used to protect the horse's legs from injury caused by **brushing.**

bucked shins   Inflammation of the shin to which young horses are particularly susceptible, once treated by **pin firing.**

bug rider   Rider who has a weight allowance; usually refers to **apprentice riders.**

bullet work   Best workout time for the distance on a given day at a track.

bull ring   Racetrack of less than one mile around.

bute   Phenylbutazone, a commonly used analgesic for horses.

ʊ C ʊ

calf-kneed   *See* **back at the knee.**

campaign   Horse's racing season.

cannon bone   Bone that extends from the knee to the **fetlock** (ankle).

capped hocks   Swelling or puffiness of the **hock,** caused by a blow or injury, or by insufficient bedding in the stable.

card   List of races offered at a given track on a given day.

cast   When a horse rolls and gets stuck either up against the stall walls or near a fence.

caulk   Projection on the bottom of horseshoes to give the horse better traction, especially on a wet track.

checked   When a horse is prohibited from running freely in a race; usually caused by interference from another horse.

chestnut   Reddish coat, with mane and tail of the same or similar color; a horse of this color.

chestnuts   Horny growths found on each of a horse's legs. The growths are located just above the knee on the front legs and just below the **hocks** on the hind legs.

chrome   Term used by auctioneers to describe the white markings of a horse.

chute   Extension of the **backstretch** or homestretch to allow a longer straight run at the start.

claimer   Horse entered in a race in which the owner is willing to sell him or her.

claiming race   Race in which all the horses entered can be purchased by a licensed owner or representative for a pre-established amount.

classic   Race exclusively for three-year-olds, such as the Kentucky Derby.

clean-legged   Horse without feathering on its lower legs.

clerk of scales   Individual responsible for verifying that each jockey carries the assigned weight, both at the start and finish of each race.

clocker   Person who times the morning workouts.

closer   Horse that runs best in the latter part of the race, coming from off the pace.

clubhouse turn   Generally, the turn immediately before the finish line and closest to the clubhouse.

coat   Horse's hide or skin.

coffin bone   Small bone within the hoof.

Coggins test   Blood test to detect **equine infectious anemia (EIA).**

colic   Medical condition marked by abdominal pain.

colors   Racing silks; jacket and cap worn by jockeys, which can be generic and provided by the track or specific to an owner.

colostrom   First milk produced by a mare following foaling.

colt   Ungelded horse under the age of five.

coming   Term used to describe the age of a horse. For example, at the age of three, a horse is said to be (U.S.) "coming three" or (England) "rising three."

conditioner   Another name for trainer.

conditioned race   Eligibility to enter is determined by a set of conditions such as age, sex, races won, and so on.

Conditioning Book   Diary of all races run at a given track during a race season, prepared by the racing secretary and containing the conditions for entry.

conformation   Physical structure of a horse.

coupled   Two or more horses running as an entry in a single betting unit.

covering   Mating of a stallion and mare.

cow hocks   When a horse has hocks located too close together and feet too far apart. Opposite of **bow hocks.** When combined with **sickle hocks,** the condition puts excessive pressure on the joint.

cracked heels   Inflammation of the heels.

crib-biting; cribbing   When a horse hooks his teeth onto something solid, such as the door of his stable, and sucks air through his open mouth.

crop   *See* **whip** and **bat.**

croup   Top of the hindquarters, from the point of the hip to the tail.

curb   Thickening of the tendon or ligament below the point of the **hock,** caused by straining.

curb bit   **Bit** that has cheeks and a **curb chain,** placed in the horse's chin groove.

curb chain A chain used with a **curb bit.**

cuppy Track's surface condition when the ground breaks away under a horse's hooves.

cyberbet Wager made via the Internet.

cyberjock Bettor who uses the Internet to wager. Also refers to a collective group that pools its funds to make exotic bets for which the guaranteed payout is at least six figures.

◡ D ◡

daily double Wager in which the bettor selects two horses that will win consecutive races; usually the first two races on the card.

Daily Racing Form Oldest newspaper dedicated to thoroughbred racing. Started in 1896 by Frank Brunnell.

daisy clipper Action of a horse that is heavy footed ("digs in" and "hugs the ground").

dam Horse's mother.

dead heat Race in which two or more horses finish in an exact tie.

dead track Racing surface that lacks resilience.

dead weight Supplemental weight added to the saddle pouch in order to reach the assigned weight for a given race.

deep going Ground that is wet or soft.

depth of girth Measurement of the **withers** to the elbow; a horse has good depth of girth when the measurement between these points is generous.

derby Stake race for three-year-olds, usually male.

dipped back Condition in which the back is hollow between the withers and the **croup,** often occurs in old age; also known as **swayback.**

dishing Action that occurs when the toe of the foreleg is thrown outward in a circular movement with each stride.

dispersal Auction in which equine holdings of a given owner are sold.

distaff Female horse of any age.

distanced When a horse is well beaten, finishing a long distance behind the winner.

dogs Wooden barriers (or rubber traffic cones) placed a certain distance out from the inner rail to protect the inner part of the track (usually the **turf course**) from traffic during workouts.

driving Strong urging by the rider.

dropped or drop noseband   Equipment that buckles beneath the bit to prevent the horse from opening its mouth to take hold of the bit and ignore the reins.

Dryland distemper   Disease that causes abscess(es) on the chest and belly; also called pigeon fever.

ʊ E ʊ

easily   Running or winning without being pressed by the jockey or opposition.

easing   Action of a jockey bringing a horse to a stop during the race, usually due to an injury or equipment problem.

engaged   Hind legs are brought well under the body.

entire   Uncastrated horse; also stallion.

entry   Two or more horses owned by the same stable or, in some cases, trained by the same trainer running as a single betting unit.

entry fee   One of the initial payments made to be eligible to compete in a given race.

equine infectious anemia (EIA)   Incurable viral disease; also known as swamp fever. *See* **Coggins test.**

equine protozoal myleoencephalitis (EPM)   A neurological disorder that invades the spinal cord and results in nerve damage.

ergot   Horny growth at the back of the **fetlock** joint.

evenly   Neither gaining nor losing position or distance during a race.

ewe neck   Defect in the horse's conformation whereby the neck appears to be upside down, or, concave along its upper edge with bulging muscles along the lower edge.

exacta   Wager in which the first two finishers in a race must be picked in exact order of finish.

exercise rider   Private contractor licensed by the track to work out horses.

exotics   Any form of multiple bet placed either on a series of races or placing positions in a given race.

extended   Forced to run at top speed.

ʊ F ʊ

faltered   When a horse that was in contention early drops back in the later stages; more drastic than *weakened*, but less drastic than *stopped*.

farrier   Blacksmith.

fast   Track condition; free of any impediments, and conducive to producing the best times.

fetlock (joint)   Lowest joint on a horse's leg.

field horse (or mutuel field)   When there are more entrants than positions on the totalizator board can accommodate and, thus, two or more starters run as a single betting unit.

figure-eight noseband   Thin leather straps that cross over at the front and buckle both above and below the **bit;** also called a grackle noseband.

filly   Female horse under the age of four.

firing   Treatment in which the skin over a leg injury is burned with a hot iron to produce scar tissue, rarely used today.

firm   Optimum condition for a **turf course,** corresponding to *fast* on a dirt track.

first turn   Bend in the track beyond the starting point.

fistulous withers   Inflamed bursar at the height of the **withers.**

flag   Signal held by a flagman standing just in front of the gate at the exact starting point of race. Official timing starts when flag is dropped.

flattens out   Horse drops its head almost on a straight line with body, generally from exhaustion.

flexion   Action of a horse yielding the lower jaw to the **bit,** with the neck bent at the poll; or the full bending of the **hock** joints (vets perform flexion tests to diagnose lameness).

flexor tendon   Tendon at the back of a horse's leg.

flying change   Change of lead at the canter or gallop performed by a horse to rebalance during turns and changes of direction.

foal   Colt, filly, or gelding up to one year of age.

forearm   Upper part of a horse's foreleg, above the knee.

forehand   Horses in early training who have not yet learned to balance themselves and are heavy in the bridle, said to be "on the forehand."

forelock   Part of the mane between the ears, which hangs forward over the forehead.

four chocolate soldiers   Horse's legs with no distinguishing markings.

frog   Triangular horny pad on the base of the hoof, which acts as a shock absorber.

frontrunner   Horse that usually leads (or tries to lead) the field as far as it can.

full card   Total number of races that will be conducted on a given day.

full mouth   Six-year-old horse with an entire set of permanent teeth.

furlong   Distance of one-eighth of a mile, or 220 yards.

furosemide   Another name for Lasix, the medication used to treat a **bleeder.**

ʊ **G** ʊ

gate   Mechanical apparatus used at the start of a race to ensure a fair and equal start.

gelding   Horse that has been castrated.

General Stud Book   European record book of all births to a registered horse on the Continent.

given its head   Refers to a horse being allowed to run freely in the pack or on the lead, without restraint by the jockey.

going   Condition of the ground, i.e., deep, good, rough.

good doer   Horse that is easy to maintain; also called thrifty.

good track   Track condition between fast and slow, generally a bit wet.

goose-rumped   Pronounced muscular development at the horse's croup; also called jumper's bump in jumpers.

graduate   Horse that has won for the first time.

graded race   Most important or prestigious races in North America; they are assigned grades (I, II, or III) based on the quality of previous winners, and the race's influence on other races or championships.

gray   Off-white, gray, or pale coat with matching mane and tail, also a horse of this color.

green   Horse that is in its early learning stages; to be green or a greenie.

groom   Person who takes direct care of one or more horses, washing, grooming, and feeding them.

ground manners   Behavior of a horse while being handled, groomed, saddled, etc.

group race   European equivalent of North American **graded races.**

☙ H ☙

handicap   Race in which weights are assigned by a racing secretary, based upon age, sex, and past performance.

handle   Total money bet on a specific race.

handily   Refers to a horse working or racing with moderate effort, but with more effort than breezing. *See* **breezing.**

hand ride   Urging a horse with the hands and arms without the jockey using the **whip.**

head of the stretch   Beginning of the straight run for the finish line.

head markings   Generally speaking, there are four types of markings: **star, stripe, snip,** and **patch,** which appear between the top of the forehead and the base of the upper lip.

heavy   Condition of track when wet, similar to **muddy** but slower.

highweight   Horse assigned the maximum weight, usually the favorite, in a **handicap race.**

hock   Hind leg joint of a horse, comparable to the human ankle.

horse   Designation given to a male horse after it has reached the age of four.

horse identifier   Person who checks the lip tattoo of each horse as it enters the paddock to verify that the correct horses are running in the race.

horse markings   Distinguishing characteristics of a horse, located in three areas: head, legs, and body.

hot blood   Horse of Arabian or Thoroughbred blood.

hot walker   Person responsible for walking horses to cool them out after workouts or races.

hung   Holding the same position during a race, unable to make up distance on the leader.

☙ I ☙

impost   Weight carried or assigned.

in hand   Running under moderate control, at less than best pace.

International Racing Bureau (Dubai World Cup)   Operational and marketing arm of the largest purse racing series in the world.

in the money   Finishing first, second, or third.

inquiry   Situation in which the track stewards review a race to check for possible infractions of the rules. Also, a sign flashed by officials on tote board on such occasions.

invitational   Stakes race open only to horses who are invited to enter. Generally, no entry fee is charged.

ʊ J ʊ

Jockey Club   The organization responsible for maintaining the American Stud Book. Consists of seven organizations: Jockey Club Interactive; Jockey Club Technology Services, Inc.; Jockey Club Racing Services, Inc.; Jockey Club Holdings, Inc.; Equity Investments & Affiliated; Grayson-Jockey Club Research Foundation, Inc.; and NYRA Investment LLC. The Jockey Club was founded in 1894.

Jockey's Guild   Organization responsible for the welfare of jockeys.

journeyman   Jockey who has advanced beyond **apprentice rider.**

ʊ L ʊ

lamintitis   Inflammation of the soft tissue inside the wall of the hoof.

lasix   Medication administered to horses. *See* **furosemide.**

leg markings   Sometimes referred to as white heel, white coronet, white pastern, white ankle half stocking, and full stocking, primarily occurring below the knee.

length   Length of a horse from head to tail (approximately eight feet).

lock   Slang term for a sure thing, a winner.

lug (in or out)   Action of a tiring horse, failing to keep a straight course, **bearing in** or out.

ʊ M ʊ

maiden   Horse that has not won a race. *See* **breaking a maiden.**

mare   Female horse that has reached the age of four.

milk shake   Slang for illegal drugs administered to a horse, usually masked by legally administered drugs.

minus pool   Mutuel pool that occurs when one horse is so heavily bet that, after deductions of state tax and commission, there is not enough money left to pay the legally prescribed minimum on each winning bet. The racing association usually makes up the difference.

morning glory   Horse who performs well in morning workouts but fails to do so in actual races.

morning line   Approximate odds quoted before wagering begins, given by the track's handicapper.

mucking out   Cleaning up a horse's stall.

mud caulks   *See* **caulks.**

muddy   Deep condition of a racetrack after being soaked with water. Horses who run well on wet tracks are generally referred to as *mudders.*

mutuel clerk   Person at the window who takes bets. Also called a *teller.*

ʊ N ʊ

National Association of State Racing Commissioners (NASRC).

National Horsemen's Benevolent and Protection Association (NHBPA)   Organization representing horsemen's interests on a myriad of issues.

National Racing Compact (NRC)   Independent, interstate governmental entity authorized by participating states and the FBI to issue national licenses for participants in horse racing with parimutuel wagering.

National Thoroughbred Racing Association (NTRA)   Organization that ensures that U.S. racing has a well-funded, national league office with programs and services that are integral to the sport's growth and development.

near side   Left side of the horse.

neck   Unit of measurement, about the length of a horse's neck, a quarter of a length.

nominating fee   Fee paid by the owner to the track to be eligible for a stakes race.

nose   Smallest margin by which a horse can win by. (In England, called a *short head.*)

ʊ O ʊ

Oaks   Stakes race for three-year-old fillies.

objection   Claim of foul lodged by rider, patrol judge, or other official. If lodged by official, it is called an **inquiry.**

odds-on   Odds of less-than-even money. In England, simply called *on;* thus, a horse "5–4 on" is actually at odds of 4–5.

official   Sign displayed when the results of a race are confirmed. Also refers to a person in a position of authority.

off the pace Horse positioned just behind the leader.

off side Right side of the horse.

on the bit Eager to run.

on the nose Betting a horse to win only.

outriders People who ride the horses that accompany racehorses to the post and who catch any racehorse that gets loose.

overbent Horse tucking his head close to his chest, limiting the rider's commands; also said to be behind the bit.

overlay Horse going off at a higher price than it appears to warrant based on his past performances.

overnight race Race in which entries close a specific number of hours before running (such as 48 hours), as opposed to a stakes race, in which nominations close far in advance.

oversubscribed Race in which the number of entrants exceeds the allowable number of starters.

overweight Surplus weight carried by a horse when the rider cannot make the assigned weight.

☙ P ❧

paddock Area in which horses are saddled and kept before post time.

pari-mutuel wagering System of wagering where all the money is returned to the wagerers after deduction of track and state percentages.

pass the box Final payment by an owner to guarantee entry into a race.

pasteboard track A lightning-fast racing strip.

patch marking Separate white or flesh-colored marking found on the upper or lower lip.

pedigree Horse's ancestry.

pick-six Wager in which the bettor attempts to select the winning horses in six consecutive races.

pin firing Method of curing **bucked shins.**

pin hooker Person who buys an untrained two-year-old horse for the purpose of resale later in the racing season.

place Second-place finish in a race.

pole Markers at measured distances around the track, signifying the distance from the finish. (The quarter pole, for instance, is a quarter of a mile from the finish, not from the start.)

pool   Mutuel pool, the total sum bet on a race or a particular bet.

post   Starting point or position in the **starting gate.**

post parade   Horses going from paddock to **starting gate,** past the grandstands.

post position   Location of stall in **starting gate** from which a horse starts.

post time   Starting time of a race. (Also, when the betting windows close.)

prep   Race or group of races deemed essential to qualifying for either a specific stake or series of stakes races.

purebred   Full-blooded member of a recognized breed.

purse   Value of a given race that will be paid to entrants based on their order of finish.

ʊ Q ʊ

quarter crack   Crack in the wall of a horse's hoof.

ʊ R ʊ

racing secretary   Employee of the race track charged with the responsibility of establishing the terms and conditions for entry into any race conducted at that track. These conditions are published in the ***Conditioning Book.***

rank   Refers to a hard-to-handle horse.

ridden out   Horse finishing a race without the rider urging him to do his utmost.

roan   Chestnut, **bay,** or sorrel sprinkled with white or gray; also a horse of this color.

route race   Race with a distance greater than a mile, usually around two turns.

rundown bandages   Wrappings placed on the hind legs, usually with pads inside, to keep a horse from scraping his heels when he runs.

ʊ S ʊ

saddle cloth   Cloth under the saddle on which the number denoting the horse's post position is displayed.

scale of weights   Fixed weights to be carried by horses in a race according to age, distance, sex, and time of year.

schooling ring   Area in which to train and exercise a horse.

scratch   To take a horse out of a race.

shadow roll   Piece of equipment that is attached to the bridle and runs across the bridge of a horse, below the eyes and above the nostrils, worn to prevent a horse from seeing shadows that might cause the animal to either jump or alter his course.

shed row   Stalls along the backstretch.

show   Third-place finish in a race.

shying   Horse moving suddenly in fright.

sickle hocks   Condition that occurs when a horse has too much of an angle in the **hock.**

side reins   Reins used in training to help position the horse's head.

silks   *See* **colors.**

simulcasting   Real-time broadcast of racing from other tracks.

sire   Horse's father.

sloppy   Track that is wet on the surface with a firm bottom.

slow   Track that has some moisture—not *fast,* between *good* and *heavy.*

snip markings   Separate white markings found between the nostrils.

sock   White markings on a horse's lower leg(s).

sophomore   Horse in its second year of racing.

splits   Various intervals of a race or workout.

spit the bit   Refers to a horse that refuses to race up to his ability.

sprint race   Race run at less than a mile, usually with only one turn.

stake   Race for which an owner must pay an entry fee. The fees can be for nominating, maintaining eligibility, entering, and starting, and are generally added to the amount put up by the track to make up the total purse.

stallion   Uncastrated horse.

star   Patch of white hair found on the horse's forehead. It can be of three shapes: diamond, star, or oval.

starter   Employee of the race track charged with the responsibility of ensuring that all the horses entered in a race are given a fair and impartial start.

starting gate   Mechanical device with stalls for horses to wait in, until the **starter** releases the doors to begin the race.

steadied   Horse being taken in hand by his rider, usually because the horse is in close quarters.

steward   Employee of the race track charged with the responsibility of ensuring that all participants adhere to the rules and regulations governing thoroughbred racing.

stick   Jockey's **whip.** (Also called a **bat.**)

stickers   **Caulks** on shoes, which give a horse better traction in mud or on soft tracks.

stocking   White markings on a horse's leg(s) that extend higher than the knee or **hock.**

stretch   Final straight portion of the racetrack to the finish line.

stretch runner   Horse that finishes fast in the final drive to the wire.

stretch turn   Bend of track into the homestretch.

stripe   Marking, that is usually white, starts at eye level, and can run down to the upper lip. If the strip includes both eyes and both nostrils, the face is considered **bald.**

stud   Stallion that is being used for breeding.

supplementary fee   Amount paid for late entry into a race. The amount can range from an additional 25 to 75 percent charge above the normal entry fee schedule.

swayback   *See* **dipped back.**

syndicate   Group of individuals who act in concert to purchase a **stallion** or **mare** for the purpose of breeding.

◡ T ◡

tack   Abbreviation of *tackle*, the original term for the equipment used in riding (saddle, bridle, etc.).

takeout   Commission deducted from mutuel pools, shared by the track and local and state governing bodies in the form of tax.

taken up   Horse pulled up sharply by his rider due to being in close quarters.

Thoroughbred Owners and Breeders Association (TOBA)   Clearinghouse of industry information for owners and breeders worldwide.

Thoroughbred Racing Association of North America (TRA)   Organization responsible for the Eclipse Awards.

tongue strap or tie   Cloth or rubber strap used to tie down a horse's tongue to prevent choking during a race or workout.

totalizator   Electronic system that calculates odds and payouts on a given race (first regular use was at Miami's Hialeah in 1932).

trainer   Person who trains and conditions the horses, is responsible for their well-being, makes decisions as to where and when they will race, and advises the owner(s) on equine matters.

Triple Crown   Coined by Charles Hatton, a writer of the ***Daily Racing Form,*** to describe three Grade I stake races for three-year-old thoroughbreds: the Kentucky Derby, the Preakness, and the Belmont.

Triple Crown Productions (TPC)   Organization responsible for nominations to the **Triple Crown,** as well as publicity.

turf course   Grass course.

ʊ U ʊ

under wraps   Horse under stout restraint in a race or workout.

ʊ V ʊ

valet   Person who takes care of a jockey's **tack** and silks, and helps him or her change for the next race.

vanned off   Horse removed from the track due to injury.

ʊ W ʊ

walkover   Horse that wins a race in which all the other competitors have withdrawn.

warming up   Galloping a horse on the way to the post.

washy   Horse breaking out in nervous sweat before a race, sometimes to the point at which sweat will be dripping from its belly.

weanling   Horse that is under the age of one, covering the first breath to becoming a **yearling.**

whip   Instrument, usually of leather, with which a rider strikes a horse to urge him on.

win   First-place finish in a race.

withers   Base of a horse's neck, attached to the shoulder, from which a horse's height is measured.

ʊ Y ʊ

yearling   Horse that is one-year-old, dating from January 1 of the year in which he was foaled.

BIBLIOGRAPHY

Alexander, David. *A Sound of Horses: The World of Racing/From Eclipse to Kelso*. Indianapolis: Bobbs-Merrill Company, Inc., 1966.

Auerbach, Ann Hagedorn. *Wild Ride: The Rise and Tragic Fall of Calumet Farm, Inc., America's Premier Racing Dynasty*. New York: Henry Holt and Company, 1994.

Beyer, Andrew. "Barrington Fair: Parsley, Sage, Rosemary, and Crime" in *My $50,000 Year at the Races*. New York: Harcourt Brace and Company, 1978.

Barich, Bill. *Laughing in the Hills*. New York: Viking Penguin, 1980.

Bolus, Jim. *Derby Fever*. Gretna, LA: Pelican Publishing Co., 1995.

Breslin, Jimmy. *Sunny Jim: The Life of America's Most Beloved Horseman, James Fitzsimmons*. Garden City, NY: Doubleday & Co., 1962.

Burick, Si. *Dayton (Ohio) Daily News*: 2 September 1955.

Cady, Steve and Barton Silverman. *Seattle Slew*. New York: Viking Penguin, 1977.

Chew, Peter. *The Kentucky Derby: The First 100 Years*. Boston, MA: Houghton Mifflin Co., 1974.

Crist, Steven. "Sorrowful Time at Claiborne Farm": *New York Times*: 1984.

Ennor, George and Bill Mooney. *The World Encyclopedia of Horse Racing: An Illustrated Guide to Flat Racing and Steeplechasing*. London: Carlton Books, 2001.

Faulkner, William. "Kentucky: Saturday: May." *Sports Illustrated*: May 16, 1955.

Flake, Carol. *Tarnished Crown: The Quest for a Racetrack Champion*. New York, NY: Doubleday & Co., 1987.

Gipe, George. *Great American Sports Book: Reminiscences of Memorable Events and Personalities in the Thrilling Story of American Sports*. Garden City, NY: Doubleday & Co., 1957.

Heinz, W. C. *Cosmopolitan:* September 1948.

Helm, Mike. *A Breed Apart: The Horses and The Players.* New York: Henry Holt and Company, 1991.

Levin, Jason. *From the Desert to the Derby: The Ruling Family of Dubai's Billion-Dollar Quest to Win America's Greatest Horse Race.* New York: Daily Racing Form Press, 2002.

Liebling, A. J. *The Honest Rainmaker: The Life and Times of Colonel John R. Stingo.* Garden City, NY: Doubleday & Co., 1953.

Lynch, Pat. *New York Journal-American:* May 5, 1957.

McEvoy, John. *Great Horse Racing Mysteries: True Tales from the Track.* Lexington, KY: Eclipse Press, 2002.

Nash, Ogden. *Selected Poetry of Ogden Nash: 650 Rhymes, Verses, Lyrics, and Poems.* New York: Black Dog & Leventhal Publishers, 1995.

Palmer, Joe H. *Saturday Evening Post:* April 1953.

_____. *This Was Racing.* New York: A. S. Barnes & Co., 1953.

Rice, Grantland. *The Tumult and the Shouting: My Life in Sport.* New York: A. S. Barnes & Co., 1954.

Ruby, Earl. *Louisville Courier-Journal:* 1957.

Runyon, Damon. *All Horseplayers Die Broke.* 1938.

Scatoni, Frank, ed. *Finished Line: A Collection of Memorable Writing on Thoroughbred Racing.* New York: Daily Racing Form Press, 2002.

Simon, Mary. *Racing Through the Century: The Story of Thoroughbred Racing in America.* Mission Viejo, CA: BowTie Press, 2002.

Smith, Red. *New York Herald-Tribune:* April 30, 1946.

_____. *New York Herald-Tribune:* January 1, 1946.

_____. *New York Herald-Tribune:* February 28, 1947.

Spink, Alfred H. *Spink Sport Stories: A Thousand Big and Little Ones,* 3 vols. The Spink Sport Stories Company, 1921.

Stump, Al. *True:* October 1958.

The Original Thoroughbred Times Racing Almanac. Mission Viejo, CA: BowTie Press, various years.

Von Borries, Philip. *Racelines: Observations on Horse Racing's Glorious History.* Masters Press, 1999.

Woods, David F. *The Fireside Book of Horse Racing.* New York: Simon & Schuster, 1963.

INDEX

ABOUT THE AUTHORS

Bert Randolph Sugar's life story sounds like a cut-and-paste job from the pages of Damon Runyon and he dresses the part, almost like a road show version of Nathan Detroit. He is seldom—some say never—seen in public without a fedora and, as often as not, smoking or chewing a cigar.

Sugar was born in Washington, D.C., a cross between the First Family of Virginia and a Hungarian pot-and-pan-peddler. Apparently his father's side of the family won out. Raised in Washington and Richmond, Sugar aspired to be an athlete, playing football, rugby, and baseball, in addition to boxing. The closest he ever came to acquitting himself in any sport was earning the reputation as "the great white *hopeless*," a backhanded reference to his amateur boxing career.

Academia beckoned . . . *repeatedly*. In his quest for higher education(!), Sugar attended Maryland, Michigan, Harvard, and American Universities, attaining various and sundry degrees. In fact, in the midst of Sugar's deciding between Harvard and Michigan, Harvard told him to go to Michigan, where he subsequently attended both law school and business graduate school.

Having graduated from Michigan with a J.D. (Doctor of Juris-prudence) and having passed the bar ("the only bar I ever passed"), Sugar opted—naturally enough—for advertising instead of law. His academic string stretched to the limit, Sugar then set his sights on New York, having adopted Willie Sutton's oft quoted raison d'être for robbing banks, "that's where the money was."

Once in New York, Sugar labored in the hallowed halls of Madison Avenue advertising firms such as McCann-Erickson; J. Walter Thompson; Papert, Koenig and Lois; D'Arcy; McManus; Masius; and others on behalf of such clients as Procter & Gamble, Warner-Lambert, Colgate, and Nestle's. Indeed, it was Bert Sugar who helped developed the now indelible ad cam-paign *N-E-S-T-L-E-S, Nestle's makes the very best . . .*

Sugar soon discovered that Madison Avenue was not for him. Perhaps it was the allure of authorship . . . the chafing of gray flannel or a donnybrook (read punch-out) of a fellow advertising executive. The fight scored more ink in *Advertising Age* than the Louis-Schmeling bout got in the *New York Times*, and Sugar de-parted the realm of advertising and entered the writing racket full time.

What he wanted to be was a sportswriter covering baseball, but he ran into a situation similar to that faced by quintessential Dodger catcher Roy Campanella. When Campanella was in high school, his coach told the prospective team members to run out to the position they wanted to play. Campanella ran to the outfield, as did about seventy other potential players. Looking back towards the bench, Campanella noticed that no one was standing behind home plate. Seeing his opportunity and seizing it, Campanella legged it back to the box, took his place behind the plate and on that day, became a catcher forever.

In Sugar's case, playing the outfield was writing about base-ball. But when he ran out on the proverbial field, he found it filled to the baselines with aspiring baseball writers. Assessing the cov-erage at the other sportswriting positions, Sugar found his "home

plate" was as a boxing writer. So there he ran, and there he stayed, becoming pugilism's premier pundit in the process.

His career includes service as editor of such magazines as the *Ring, Boxing Illustrated, Argosy, Baseball Monthly, Gridiron, Basketball News,* and *Fight Game.* And while his famous fedora and cigar are ringside fixtures as much as the ref, the bell, and the end-swell, Sugar's countenance is becoming familiar to an increasingly wider audience of moviegoers and television viewers. To date, he has appeared on ESPN and HBO and in such films as *Night and the City* with Robert DeNiro, *The Great White Hype* with Samuel L. Jackson, *Play It to the Bone* with Woody Harrelson and Antonio Banderas, and on television in HBO's hit series *Arliss.*

Bert is a columnist for *SportsBusiness Journal* and is a contributing editor to several publications including *Smoke Magazine, Irish Connections, Glasgow Sunday Herald,* and *S.A. Sports Illustrated.* He and his wife make their home in Westchester County, New York.

Cornell Richardson is a native New Yorker who, by his own admission, was raised in the shadows of the long-defunct Jamaica Race Track and spent many a morning before school working along the backstretch. His fascination with racing continued throughout his school years, which included a degree from St. John's University and an MBA from Columbia. (As a gift for his having graduated Columbia, his wife gave him a Currier & Ives print of a horse named Tenny, circa 1890, to celebrate both his graduation and his love of horses.) Early in his career, Richardson was a major lending officer at major banking institutions (Chemical and National Westminster), where he serviced the entertainment and sports industries, including many of those in the

racing industry. Later, he represented sports personalities and produced and wrote several television sports programs. Currently, he is working with renowned TV director and documentarian Bud Greenspan on a documentary on horse racing for ESPN, as well as coauthoring a book titled *The Ladies Wore Silks: The History of Women in Thoroughbred Racing.*

ABOUT THE ARTIST

As a sports artist and chronicler of contemporary lifestyles, and as a creator of the subject of action, **LeRoy Neiman** has become as familiar as the well-known sports heroes and international personalities he paints. His is the work of an artist who paints the people and events of the world he knows best, and which truly captures the look and feel of that world. Neiman's work has been influenced by the art of Toulouse-Lautrec, Dufy, and the New York Social Realists, who have affected his choice of subject matter.

His colors are brilliant and raw, and their spontaneous application also reflects the influence of the Abstract Expressionists on his work. Through his unique style, he has brought figure painting and social realism to the public from the frenzied 1950s to today.

Neiman, having the ability to draw quickly and grasp the moment, has become the recorder of the exciting events affecting American life in our time.

PERMISSIONS

The publisher acknowledges the following for permission to reproduce copyrighted material:

Getty Images/Getty Images North America for the photographs that appear on pages: ii (frontispiece), 12, 34, 42, 76, 107, 144.

The Hulton Archive for prints and photographs that appear on pages xiv, 100, 126.

Mary Evans Photo Library for the print on page 7.

The Jockey Club for tables appearing on pages 32, 65, 152, 156, 159, 161.

A portion of the poem "Hoppy New Year" on page 139 is copyright © 1950 by Walter W. Smith and reprinted courtesy of Curtis Brown, Ltd. from Red Smith, *Out of the Red*, Knopf: New York, 1950.

Every attempt has been made to contact copyright holders. Any omissions will be corrected in future editions.